HANGING UP THE ROPE

PAUL HUEBNER

Lovstad Publishing
Poynette, Wisconsin

ISBN: 0615948030
ISBN-13: 978-0615948034

Printed in the United States of America

Cover design by Lovstad Publishing
Cover photo by Lenore Sobota: Author at top of
Old Man's Dome, South Dakota Needles

Dedicated to Judy Huebner

PAUL HUEBNER

ACKNOWLEDGMENTS

I'd like to thank several former Jackson Hole Mountain Guides, in particular, Jay Pistono and former owners, Andy Carson and Paul Horton for their friendship and instruction in a number of climbing classes and guided ascents in the Grand Tetons.

Jim Ebert (now deceased) for making me a rope leader in the former Iowa Mountaineering Club, and Andy Petefish for giving me the opportunity, guidance and confidence to lead teams up three of the adjacent peaks to Mt. Assiniboine.

I will always remember Hans Steyskal for his persistence in convincing me to join him on the challenging climb of the Southwest Ridge of the Zinal Rothorn. That particular climb and our epic descent back to Zermatt in the dark still stands above all others, including my ascent of the Matterhorn just two days prior, as the most spectacular and demanding day I've spent in the European Alps.

I also want to acknowledge former Colorado Mountain School (CMS) Guide, Mike Caldwell, who led me to my personal high point -- the 21,205-foot summit of Nevado Illimani in Bolivia, and CMS Guide, Marko Cornacchione, who I first met in Mexico City. Marko's contagious enthusiasm made the Mexican Trilogy Expedition one of my most enjoyable trips. He also further strengthened my rock climbing lead skills at Lumpy Ridge above Estes Park, Colorado.

Alaska Mountain School founder, Colby Coombs needs to be recognized for pushing me beyond my comfort zone and for relentlessly demanding the speed and efficiency necessary for safe passage in the great ranges. It was Colby's instruction that provided me the skill to react so quickly to arrest Alaska Mountaineering and Climbing School Head Guide Sean Gaffney's fall, when he dropped into a hidden crevasse on the slopes of Mt. Bona in the Wrangell/St. Elias Range in Alaska.

I'd like to thank Matt Schonwald for his companionship and for convincing me to ascend the difficult Entiat Icefall.

And, of course, I want to thank all of the others that have shared the brotherhood of the rope with me, in particular my former climbing partners John Pruessner, David Panofsky, and especially the other members of the "Rushmore Gang" -- Lenore Sobota, Anne Meyer, and David Meyer.

Last, but certainly not least, I want to acknowledge my family and most especially my lovely wife Judy. She has put up with my obsession for adventure, the related injuries I incurred, and continues to encourage me to pursue most of my dreams.

CONTENTS

PAUL HUEBNER

HANGING UP THE ROPE

FOREWORD
By Craig Spychalla

Paul Huebner can tell you what it's like to stand with the world beneath his feet, with only blue sky above.

He can describe what it was like to be greeted by a hotel clerk holding a shotgun in Ecuador during an uprising against the government. He can even recall the time he was hallucinating on a mountain in Bolivia because of altitude sickness. He can do all this while letting others understand the feeling that rushes through his body as he climbs to the summit of his next adventure. And only then do you begin to truly understand why he does it.

I met Paul more than a decade ago when he asked if I would be interested in a story for the paper about his latest climbing adventure. I said sure, not knowing much about climbing myself. What Paul turned in wasn't just a story about climbing, his story was about one person's journey to the top of the world, his world – and he took others and me along for an incredible ride.

For more than two decades, Paul has been leaving his Portage, Wisconsin, home to climb mountains around the world and share stories of his adventures in local newspapers. To him, climbing mountains is not about conquering them. It's about camaraderie with other climbers who hold his life in their hands. It's about a majestic view, one that can only be experienced at 20,000 feet. And it's about figuring out how to deal with what nature will throw at him next.

This is a guy who even in his 60s biked and walked 20 miles a day, and did short climbs and long hikes to stay in shape for his next trip to places most of us only see in magazines. Many of us have thought about taking an adventure trip to spice up our lives. But Paul has lived that philosophy. After he climbs one mountain, there's always another he is setting his sights on.

In his latest project, "Hanging up the rope," Paul takes you on a ride unlike many others, introducing us to climbing friends and parts of America, and the world, most of us will never see – at least not like this. There are crevasses in the snow, rocks that tumble only feet away. Lives are lost, and ones are found on mountainsides. This book is a different look at the scenic views of the world. While the average person is looking at the mountain from the ground, there are few people like Paul who are looking back.

Throughout the book, we find Paul making trips, like short ones to Devil's Lake in Baraboo, not far from his home, to unforgettable jaunts to Bolivia, Ecuador, and Mexico and getting immersed into the local cultures. While the mountains pose their own challenges, so does the journey to foreign lands, including the threat of an airlines strike and ousting of a country's corrupt President. What makes this book much more than one climber talking about his passion is the places we visit and stay, like the Magic Bean while drinking some Scottish beer with friends.

While most children have dreams of riding the Matterhorn at Disneyland, Paul had the idea of climbing the real thing at that age, and achieving that in 1990.

Hanging Up The Rope puts you next to Paul as he looks down at the climbers below, like marching ants heading to the West Face of the Marmolata in the Italian Dolomites. And you share the joys of success on the summit before heading to the Matterhorn, with a cheese sandwich and some wine to wash things down.

The Matterhorn is a different test, with never-ending rock and snow in front of him. As fatigue sets in, we find out what true determination these climbers have. But the peak is only the halfway point – there's the climb down where accidents often occur. And here we find out that one climber on this trip did not succeed, with the drama of the fallen playing out before our eyes. We are reminded of the great danger that comes in wanting to see the world from a different view. But for these climbers, these men and women of the mountains, the risk is worth a reward that keeps us all spellbound at what will happen next.

Craig Spychalla is a journalist for the *Portage Daily Register*

INTRODUCTION
By Lenore Sobota

Paul Huebner and I first met on a long – very long – van ride to British Columbia in 1988 to climb in the Purcells with the Iowa Mountaineers. Little did I know the adventures - and misadventures -- we would share in the decades that followed.

Paul already had done a fair bit of climbing before that journey to the Purcells, and he was just getting started. In the pages of this book, he relates many of his incredible journeys.

He didn't let living in the relative flatland's of Wisconsin prevent him from finding his place in the mountains. His climbing took him to the Alps of Europe, mountains of Alaska, the Colorado Rockies, Canada and the North Cascades, the volcanoes of Mexico and to the Andes of Bolivia and Ecuador. Yet, he didn't let those far-flung travels to classic peaks prevent him from finding beauty and challenge on the rocks of Wyoming, Colorado, South Dakota and even in his backyard of Devils Lake, Wisconsin.

Along the way, he saw how fragile life in the mountains can be and had a few close calls of his own. Like many climbers, he pondered the question of life and death and "why I climb." There are as many reasons to climb, as there are climbers. It's a question most of us ask at one time or another, often after a close call or witnessing an accident but also while shivering in the rain or cold (or both) – or driving across the unchanging landscape of Saskatchewan in the summer heat, crammed in a poorly ventilated van with a bunch of strangers and no mountains in sight. But those strangers become friends – friends in whom you literally trust your life.

While many team sports or other athletic endeavors foster camaraderie, few involve the level of trust required in climbing when you tie yourself to another and count on them to catch you if you fall.

In these pages, you will meet some of the people in whom Paul has placed that trust – and who have put their trust in Paul. Some of the best days in the mountains or on the rocks have little to do with reaching the summit or high point and everything to do with spending time with friends; sharing your thoughts and, yes, even fears; working together as a team and celebrating your partners' triumphs as well as your own.

That's why "hanging up the rope" can be difficult for a climber to do. Climbing is not just something we do; it's part of who we are. But while a rope can be untied, the ties that bind old climbing partners together remain even after hanging up the rope.

HANGING UP THE ROPE

ANOTHER TRAGEDY
ON THE MATTERHORN

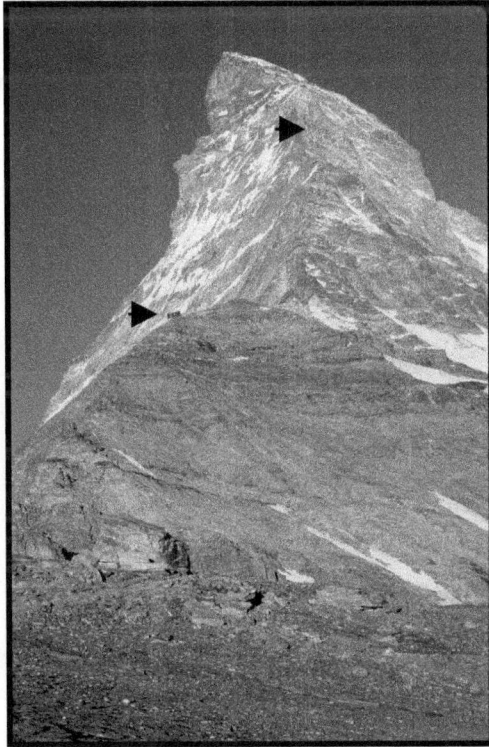

Lower arrow points out location of the Hörnli Hut and the upper arrow indicates the East Ridge on the Matterhorn. (Photo by author)

We all have secret hopes and ambitions. One of mine since grade school was to one day ascend the most famous and glamorous peak in the Alps. My opportunity to climb the Matterhorn came in 1990, when my wife Judy and I signed up for the Iowa Mountaineers European Outing. The trip was the 50th Anniversary celebration of the mountaineering club's founding.

The normal or easiest route up the Matterhorn is the East Ridge. It's a relatively long, easy climb in fair weather. Armed with this knowledge numerous climbers underestimate the seriousness of the ascent every year, and far too many lives (10 to 12) have been lost on the quintessential Alp annually. While descending from the Matterhorn's summit, the tragic death of yet another climber on its slopes profoundly affected my exuberance of having attained my goal.

Nineteen of us from the Midwest departed O'Hare in a Lufthansa 747 on June 30. Eight hours and a day later, Iowa Mountaineering Club founder John Ebert and his son Jim greeted us at the Munich airport.

They quickly divided us up into six smaller groups. Each group was then assigned to a brand new, rented Volkswagen van. Having previous experience as a participant and rope leader on other trips with the club, I was one of the designated drivers. We traveled in a caravan to the Hotel Stachus, and when we arrived Jim introduced us to three guides and 12 other participants who had arrived from the states on an earlier flight.

We all spent the next day in the carefree "Bavarian world-city," sightseeing and doing a little shopping on our own.

The following morning we traveled to the Hohe Tauren National Park in Austria. Our destination was the Hotel Glocknerhaus located near the idyllic, Alpine village of Heiligenblut. The two-story mountain inn overlooks the Grossglockner, which at 12,500 feet is the highest Alp in Austria.

While driving on the Autobahn I quickly learned to avoid pulling out into the fast lane. I'd look in the van's rearview and side mirrors, and there would be no traffic whatsoever behind me. Then just as I'd begin to edge over towards the adjacent passing lane a big Mercedes would unfailingly appear on the road far behind us and close the gap between us in seconds.

That evening in the Glocknerhaus dining room Jim introduced us to six Austrian Guides who would be joining us. Four of the six had guided for the club on past outings to the Alps. Two of the Austrians, Zepp Zink and Herwig Habenbacher rode with my van. Zepp rode shotgun and I appreciated his navigational assistance and driving advice. While traveling the narrow mountain roads in Austria I was amazed how the European drivers would aggressively pass even on blind curves, and some of the oncoming drivers would even play chicken with us. I'm sure that my American passengers closed their eyes a number of times when I had to stomp on the gas or brakes and perform a last minute maneuver to avoid a collision. I eventually adapted and drove almost as crazy as the locals.

Rain and a sharp breeze greeted us on the morning of July 4 in the parking lot at the Glocknerhaus. Our itinerary for the day called for a break-in hike from Heiligenblut back up to the Alpine hotel -- a distance of 14.2 kilometers or about 8.5 miles.

By afternoon the cold rain turned to a wet, sticky snow. But our enjoyment of the postcard scenery that surrounded us wasn't dampened. After everybody returned to the Glocknerhaus we were divided into two large groups -- those who came to go on day hikes and those of us who came to climb. The climbers were then further split up into two smaller groups.

The next day the climbers left shortly after breakfast to ascend up to the Erzherzog-Johann Hut, which is perched on a saddle of the Grossglockner at 11,322 feet. Each group took a different route.

My group drove back down to Heiligenblut and around to the backside of the Grossglockner to a trailhead located above the small village of Kals. From there it's a longer, but initially easier approach to the climbers hut than the steeper and shorter route the other group planned to ascend directly up from the other side of the Pasterze Glacier. The colossal glacier is situated right below the large, circular car park at the end of the road above the Glocknerhaus.

Clouds began to form in the valleys far below us as we proceeded up the mountain. The route from the Kals Trailhead leads across a wide, sloping snowfield that borders a huge, sheer drop off. The clouds soon overtook us and it began to snow just as we were crossing the snowfield. Blinded by whiteout conditions we endured a terrifying moment in the poor visibility, when we heard a growing rumble indicating an avalanche was occurring somewhere above us. Helplessly roped together we stopped in our tracks, collectively held our breaths, and anticipated the worst. We were quite relieved when the slide stopped shortly after it had started.

On the other side of the snowfield the route to the hut leads up a somewhat difficult and steep rocky ridge. The wind increased exponentially just as we began to ascend it, and it became nearly impossible to verbally communicate with each other.

Tied in behind Zepp, who was leading our group, I was being whipsawed. Each time someone below me stumbled, stopped, or just had trouble keeping up with Zepp's pace the Austrian would haul on the rope and shout back at me in German to keep moving. I was totally exasperated. When Zepp and I finally topped out onto the level ground of the high saddle the hut is situated on, I immediately untied from the tormenting rope and stomped off to the two-story building.

I found the common room on the first floor of the building absolutely packed with several other climbers seeking shelter from the storm and the members of our other group, who had arrived ahead of me. The dark and damp room actually reminded me of a cave—water dripped from man-made stalactites composed of wet boots, socks, and other clothing suspended from the low ceiling's exposed rafters. But what a tremendous relief it was to get in out of the windblown horizontal snow and cold.

I purchased a large mug of raspberry tea and a hot bowl of mashed potatoes, then made my way through the crowd to the pot-bellied stove located in a back corner of the room to thaw out my fingers and toes.

After inhaling a second cup of tea I checked out the upstairs sleeping quarters and regretted not having gone up the narrow stairs immediately after my arrival. Others from my climbing group had already claimed the remaining double level sleeping platforms that exist on both sides of the dormitory-like room. Just when it looked like I was going to be sleeping on the floor with others that still hadn't come upstairs, Jim Ebert magically appeared through a small door and offered, "Paul, you can join me if you want. There's an empty place inside my room." Jim had obviously reserved the small, private room before leaving the Glocknerhaus. I jumped at the opportunity thinking I was actually going to get a much needed good night's rest after all. Ironically, I spent the entire night listening to violent gusts of wind shake every beam and rafter of the hut, the machine gun rat-a-tat of graupel bouncing off of the room's one tiny windowpane, and Jim's legendary snoring.

The violent storm was still raging at 5:00 a.m. when Jim had gotten up to check things out. I soon decided to crawl out of my cozy sleeping bag to see what he planned to do and was surprised to see that nobody else in the dorm room appeared to be getting ready to go anywhere. Most were still asleep. Right then Jim came back upstairs and told me he had already called off the climb.

Then before I could turn around and go back to bed Jim asked me to join him downstairs. I was surprised to see Zepp dressed and waiting there. Jim had decided that the three of us should descend back to the trailhead above Kals and drive the two vans we had left there back up to the car park above the Glocknerhaus. His plan made sense because the route down to the Pasterze Glacier provides the quickest way off of the mountain, and the outing itinerary called for spending the next two nights at a mountain inn in the Italian Dolomites.

A big metal latch secures the Erzherzog-Johann Hut's heavy wooden outside door. I lifted the bar-like latch and cracked the door open against the wind to see if there was even a hint of blue in any direction in the sky. Horizontal sleet stung my eyes and all I saw when I looked up was a mass of boiling, gray-black clouds. I returned upstairs and put on every spare piece of clothing I had in my pack.

When the three of us left, Zepp led, Jim was tied into the middle of the rope, and I was attached at the rear. Zepp bypassed the steep section of the route we had ascended below the saddle the previous afternoon. Instead he continued straight ahead to a narrow opening between two large rock buttresses.

After passing through the gap we encountered a ramp leading up along a vertical wall of shale. The ramp covered with sharp-edged standing plates of the weathered sedimentary rock resembled the back of a prehistoric stegosaurus. There was an extreme void filled with darkness and swirling snow to our left that looked like the virtual edge of the earth.

Tremendous gusts of wind slammed into us with astonishing speed and power as we traversed the exposed ramp. If taken by surprise they could clearly have blown us off of our feet.

In the blinding snow I focused like a laser on Jim's silhouette. Being so much lighter than Jim each time I saw him stop and struggling to stay upright I knew it was time for me to crouch down on one knee, jam my ice axe into a rock crevice, and hang on for dear life. I just knew that if I were ripped off of the ramp, the rope would surely snag on one of the sharp-edged slabs of shale and probably be cut as Jim and Zepp arrested my fall.

We continued to fight our way along the ramp until we came to a slot in the vertical rock wall that leads down a steep snow chute between two descending rock ridges. We quickly reached the bottom of the chute, turned the corner around the base of the rock ridge on our right and encountered the avalanche-primed bowl we had traveled across the day before. This time, while post-holing across it I felt like one of those little targets slowly moving along the mechanized track in the back of a shooting gallery at the county fair. It took us what seemed like an eternity to make our way to the rocky path on the other side of it. The clouds than finally began to shred apart and the ferocity of the wind lessened more and more as we progressed further down the mountain.

The vicious storm finally released its brutal grip on the upper mountain later that morning, and a couple of our more experienced climbers along with some of the American and Austrian Guides used the window of opportunity to nab the Grossglockner's summit.

Back at the Glocknerhaus that evening I jealously queried Hans Steyskal, one of the American guides who participated on the successful climb, what the route above the hut was like. "It's not that difficult," he said. I then expressed my disappointment on missing out on the climb. Steyskal just smiled and crowed, "In the mountains the early bird doesn't always get the worm."

Early the next morning we left to drive to the Rifugio Auronzo, which is a large, modern refuge located in the Italian Dolomites just above the Olympic City of Torino. The building is situated right below the impressive towers of the famous Tre Cima (Drei Zinnen if your Austrian) within the Tre Cima di Lavaredo Natural Park. You can still see bunkers dug into the rock ramparts and discover spent shells from old battles that occurred within the park's boundaries during World War I when Austria lost the Tyrol Region to Italy.

There also still seems to still be hard feelings between the two countries. Our van's pool of Lira for gas and other miscellaneous expenses took a big hit when Zepp argued with the park personnel attending the gate over what appeared to be an exorbitant tariff for admission to the park. We finally just paid what they demanded and, then unbelievably two days later, the same guards would not open the gate for us to leave the park without providing them additional Lira. When I questioned Herwig, who could speak English how they could do that, he just smirked and said, "They just want the money to purchase a bottle of wine."

While staying at the park the hikers and the less experienced climbers scrambled up a couple of high points. The rest of us ascended two of the Tre Cima -- the Cima Piccolo (Kleine Zinnen) and Cima Grande (Grosse Zinnen).

Loose rocks and pebbles lay on every little edge and ledge of the extremely weathered limestone. Hans Steyskal led Jesse Glidden and I up a moderately difficult route to the summit of the Cima Piccolo, and Jesse's father American Guide Jock Glidden led another rope team of three below us. The hardest part of the climb was making sure not to dislodge any of the loose debris, while moving almost directly above our companions, and having to descend frozen steps in the snow without crampons after we had rappelled down from the summit into the steep notch between the Cima Piccolo and Cima Grande.

Streamers of fog swirled around us halfway up the Cima Piccolo climb. Idle chatter and occasional laughter from hikers on the maze of trails below filtered up to us, but for the most part it was so still and quiet we could hear even the smallest pebbles drop. Simultaneously, American Guide Bob Wilson was leading the first of two rope teams ascending an easier route up the higher and adjacent Cima Grande. Bob has a deep radio voice, and while virtually smothered in the fog, he boomed, "This is God speaking!" You had to be there.

View above the clouds from the Cima Piccolo summit
(Photo by author)

23

Austrian Guide Hans Jantscher, Wayne Baker and I romped up the same route to Cima Grande's summit the next day. Head Austrian Guide and famous World War II flying ace Kurt Hofer and a lawyer named Jim Craig from the State of Washington soon joined us. Craig was celebrating his 69th birthday.

Wayne joined Kurt and Jim, while I soloed the descent. On my way down the climb I met an Italian Guide, who was leading a client up the climb. He didn't seem happy that he had to wait for me to pass him by. Then several feet above me he or his clumsy client accidentally dislodged a fairly large rock. They didn't call out a warning, and when it bounced past me it just barely missed me. I lodged a rather loud compliant, and the Guide with his back to me just shrugged, raised his right arm into the air and mocking said over his shoulder in English, "That's climbing in the mountains!"

On July 10 we moved on to the Rufugio Dolomia, which is nestled directly beneath the mighty Marmolada. The massive snow and glacier clad mountain known as the "Queen of the Dolomites" rises to 10,295 feet.

I came down with a bad cold that evening. The next day the climbers ascended the Queen's snowy East Ridge, while I had to spend it with the hikers. We spent the entire morning hiking up to the Rifugio Padon, which is located on top of the high ridge directly across from Marmolata. My gaze was constantly drawn to the overpowering view of the mountain and each time I strained to see the climbers on the East Ridge. The hikers definitely seemed to be having more fun than us more serious climbers. Still, I longed to be suffering on the mountain with my fellow climbers.   The restroom at the Rifugio Pardon helped lift my spirits. In Europe every indoor toilet we encountered seemed to have a different flushing mechanism, and it generally was a challenge to discover where it was located. I had a cleaning maid mop between my legs, while I was making use of a public urinal in Munich. But my experience using the restroom in the Rifugio Padon is even more memorable. The unique, unisex facility is a rather large room on the lower level of the two-story building. Its floor is a shallow, sloping stainless steel like tub with an open hole in its center. There is a slightly elevated, non-slip corrugated footpad on each side of the hole and when squatting over the hole with your boots strategically placed on the pads you need to reach up and pull a chain suspended from the ceiling to flush. A large volume of water then rushes out from holes in the baseboard of the walls of the room, swirls around your feet, and forms a small whirlpool as it drains through the hole. I was laughing so hard at the whole show I almost failed to keep my boots dry.

One of the hiking guides from Austria was named Hubie Schlapschi. His somewhat younger brother Karl and Karl's lady friend Helga joined us at the Rufugio Dolomia for dinner that evening. Karl doesn't speak English, but he managed to captivate the entire room with his loud voice, belly laugh and party-loving personality. Both during and after dinner he drank voluminous amounts of wine. After eating and accompanied by Kurt on his guitar he sang songs with the rest of his countrymen.

Helga, unlike Karl, speaks very good English. I was sitting next to her, and she leaned over and whispered to me, "Karl is 68 years old and had triple-bypass heart surgery last year...his doctors told him he should quit climbing, but the two of us just returned from ascending several peaks up to 20,000 feet high in Peru." She took a sip of wine and then boasted, "Karl takes great pride in proving his doctors wrong...he's preparing to go to the Himalayas this fall to see just how high he can go."

The Austrian Guides knew how disappointed I was in missing out on yet another mountain summit. Apparently Kurt discussed my skills and situation with Karl, because as the evening began to grow a little long in the tooth, Kurt came over to me and asked if I'd like to join Karl and Helga in the morning to ascend Marmolata. I was at first speechless. It was a very gracious offer, but our entire group was leaving in the morning for the Olympian Village of Madonna di Campiglio. Kurt realizing my concern assured me that Karl would drive me to our next accommodation after our climb. I was still reluctant to be the third wheel on the climb with Karl and Helga. I felt I'd be intruding, but they both made me feel very welcome. When Judy nodded her approval, I excitedly agreed to team up with them.

The three of us ascended the Queen's sheer West Face on *via ferrata* —iron ladder rungs installed into the featureless limestone. Picture a 3,000-foot high water tower with no metal cage wrapped around its ladder. You can then imagine what the exposure is like on the climb. When I looked down, other roped climbers traversing the glacier far below us to the start of the route looked like lines of foraging ants.

Ascending *via ferrata* on the West Face of Marmolata. Note climbers approaching on the glacier below. (Photo by author)

Upon reaching the one-room, rickety hut located atop her Majesty's crown Karl insisted that we celebrate our successful ascent by enjoying a cheese sandwich and more importantly a good bottle of wine to wash it down.

Before descending the East Ridge, Karl nonchalantly instructed me to jump off the opposite side of the razor-edged snowy ridge if he should slip. I thought he was joking, but then quickly realized such a drastic, countering maneuver might actually stop a rope team from plunging all the way down to the glacier below.

Two hours later we were barreling through the winding Adige Valley at 190 kilometers (about 114 mph) in Karl's powerful Mercedes sedan. Sitting in the back seat I felt safer climbing Marmolata. While racing through the narrow, cobbled streets of small northern Italian villages Helga sensed my concern, turned around in the front seat, and laughed just as Karl's tires squealed around a very tight corner. Then with a light pat on his right shoulder, she announced "Don't worry Paul, Karl is an excellent driver." It was like flying, my safety was totally out of my control. I just decided to relax and look out the window to watch the beautiful Italian countryside whip by.

The next day at our hotel in Madonna di Campiglio my head cold returned, and it kept me from joining the climbers, when they left that morning in two groups to explore the Adamello-Brenta Natural Park for three days. Meanwhile, I needed to nurse myself back to health before challenging the higher and more physically demanding Eastern Alps. I spent the next two days leading some hikes into the magnificent backcountry of the park with Judy and a small group of our hikers.

During that time the climbers made successful ascents of Cima Brenta and Cima Tosa, the two highest peaks in the Brenta Region at 10,410 and 10,335 feet, respectively. A select few also scaled the more difficult Campanile Basso, a dolomitic pinnacle over 800 feet tall, that has a large bell installed on its 10,074-foot high summit.

I enjoyed the company of the hikers, but when the climbers returned a day early due to stormy weather and boasted about their successful ascents over the previous two days I started feeling sorry for myself, especially for having missed out on the rock climb up the Campanile Basso.

We left the small resort town on July 16 for Zermatt, Switzerland. Autos are banned in Zermatt, but a train provides transportation from Täsch -- a mere distance of five kilometers or about three miles. Upon our arrival at the Zermatt Railway Station we obtained a lift to our assigned hotels on electric-powered carts. Leaving the train station on board one of the unique and silent running cabs I immediately searched the 14,000-foot high peaks surrounding the village for that first glimpse of the famous Matterhorn.

Rounding a curve in the road I wasn't prepared for the view that confronted me. Penetrating the sky like a frozen candle flame, the isolated Alp looks so steep that I was instantly intimidated. I actually had to look away to gather back my scattered confidence.

A week earlier Zermatt celebrated the 125th Anniversary of the first ascent of the Matterhorn. In 1865, Edward Whympher and a party of six other men were the first to scale the ominous looking Alp. In a tragic fall four of Whympher's companions, including his Swiss Guide, died when their rope broke while descending from the steep summit. Part of the festivities included a climb of the historic route up the East Ridge by a group of well-known mountaineers from all over the world. There were still so many alpinists and tourists in the renowned resort that members of our group had to stay in three different hotels. That evening only eight of us out of the 20 climbers in our group were picked to ascend the Matterhorn with six of our guides. Herwig Habenbacher, a bashful 21-year-old engineering student from Eisenerz, Austria, was my assigned guide and rope partner.

Jim Ebert and the fourteen of us took the Luftseibahn (cable car) from Furi up to the Hotel Schwarzee the very next afternoon. We then hiked up to the Hörnli Hut from the Schwarzee Platform to spend the night.

The well-worn path to the historic hut leads over 40 switchbacks and I became more impressed with the sheer bulk and height of the Matterhorn with each step upward. It took me about two hours to reach the hut, which is located just below the base of the East Ridge at an elevation of 10,693 feet. After catching my breath, I dallied on the stone terrace outside the shelter just long enough to take in the magnificent and uninterrupted view of the Alps that encircle Zermatt and the Visptal Valley to the north. A strong, cold wind discouraged me from attempting to enjoy and photograph the colorful pink Alpen-glow that promised to develop on the steep barrier that divides Switzerland from Italy -- the massive Monte Rosa Group.

Inside the first floor and common room of the hut I found the rest of my companions congregated together on benches drawn up to two long, wooden tables. Like several other hopeful climbers in the hut, they were sipping either hot tea or a cold beer.

A young French woman dispensed our dinner from huge steel kettles, and I had two servings of everything knowing it would be my last hot meal until the following evening after the climb.

Shortly after eating and knowing that we'd be leaving in darkness I retired upstairs to find my assigned bunk, while there was still some daylight left to organize my gear.

On the Matterhorn, it's imperative that you get as early an "Alpine Start" as possible. Your penalty for oversleeping is to spend much of your climb dodging rock fall loosened by parties above you. You also would need to wait for them to advance and make way for them when they descend, while you're still trying to reach the summit. It usually takes mere mortals about 10-12 hours to make the round trip from the hut to the summit and back.

I was still wide-awake at 4:00 in the morning from anticipation and had to relieve myself. Getting to the Hörnli Hut's outhouses is a harrowing experience in the dark, even with a headlamp. Privies are located around the back of the building and the access to them is a two-foot wide, snow and ice covered path with a sheer drop off of over a thousand feet adjacent to it. The only protection provided is a single strand of wire cable strung through a couple of steel poles seated in concrete alongside the edge of the cliff. I couldn't help ponder whether any of the hundreds of Matterhorn deaths resulted from a slip while traveling to or back from the outhouses.

Shortly after hearing the Zermatt Guides and their clients stirring, Herwig and I were stumbling along behind some of them on the start of the route by headlamp. We climbed steadily for more than an hour before a sliver of red demarking the skyline was the first indication that night was yielding to dawn.

We hadn't roped up yet, because the route initially consists of just steep scrambling, mixed with easy vertical sections and a few narrow ledges. Then as you round a corner and enter a steep gully the climbing becomes steady and continuous, but it's still just hard enough to remain interesting.

On the Gibiss, steep rock slabs leading up to the Untere Moseley Platte (Lower Moseley rocks), the angle of ascent never seemed to let up, and I made a mental note of how hard it was going to be coming back down facing out from the rock. But at that point I was still quite comfortable continuing on without using the rope.

High, isolated peaks like the Matterhorn make their own weather and a few wispy clouds began to form below us when we reached the Solvay Hut. The so-called hut is a very small emergency concrete shelter constructed at an elevation of 13,100 feet. We took a short break there to consume some needed calories.

We finally attached ourselves to our rope and, just as on the Grossglockner, the clouds rose up the mountainside. They engulfed us up on the perpendicular Obere Moseley Platte (Upper Moseley rocks). The section is named after the American Edward Moseley, who perished there in 1869. A slight wind occasionally parted the swirling vapors and revealed the route ahead or even a more distant view. But otherwise, I could barely make out Herwig in his red parka only a short distance above me. The clinging mists finally were stalled by a stiff North Westerly above the Untere Roterturm (Lower Red Tower) rocks.

Spindrift replaced the cloud cover when the two of us mounted the

Schultergrat (Shoulder Ridge). We stopped there to put crampons on our boots before crossing the ridge to the Oberer Roterturm (Upper Red Tower) rocks that lead to fixed ropes placed on the edge of the North Face, where the first accident occurred in 1865.

At that point on the route the rock is vertical to overhanging and you have to literally haul yourself up a thick, fixed rope -- think of the rope you may have had to climb back in high school gym class. I removed and put away my crampons and began the strenuous task of ascending the rope hand over hand while walking my feet up the rock. Suddenly the coarse rope was causing the cuffs of my thin liner gloves to roll up the palms of my hands. Before losing my grip I stopped and peeled them off one at a time with my teeth. My exposed fingers were then instantly numbed by the icy cold wind, and when I finally reached the top of the rope I had lost all feeling in my fingertips. They were pearly white and I was sure they were frostbitten.

I quickly removed my pack, retrieved my insulated gloves, slipped them on and frantically began to vigorously windmill my arms. I was very relieved to feel my blood begin to seep back into my fingers, even though it felt like I was holding them over an open flame.

We put our crampons back on, and shortly after we recommenced climbing other faster parties were already descending from the summit. From then on, the dreaded two-way traffic impeded our progress. Having to wait at a couple of the belay stances for others to clip into and out of the anchors as they passed by, I placed a hand over my locking carabiner to protect it from being accidentally loosened or even un-clipped. I was shocked speechless when one climber actually used my helmet for a foothold.

The final snow ridge to the summit seemed never-ending. Every time I dared to take my eyes off of my feet and look up after surmounting what I had thought was going to be the summit; another false one replaced it. The combination of altitude, cold, fatigue and disappointment began to erode my determination.

It was 10:00 a.m., when I noticed two climbers standing off to my right. Another was approaching a huge iron cross a little below the elevation where I stood with Herwig from a different route.

Climbers returning to the Matterhorn's Swiss summit from its lower Italian summit and another climber is approaching the iron cross on the Italian summit. (Photo by author)

Slowly the synapses in my brain registered that Herwig and I were actually just below the knife-edge ridge leading to the higher 14,690-foot high Swiss Summit.

I sat down in the snow when we reached the summit cross and took three quick photographs -- one of Herwig, one of the ridge leading down to the Italian Summit, and another of the splendid view of the Ober Gabelhorn, the Zinal Rothorn (the Red Fortress), and the perfect pyramid of the Weisshorn marching off to the northeast.

View to the east from the Matterhorn summit of the Gabelhorn, Zinal Rothorn, and Weisshorn. (Photo by author)

Herwig offered to take a picture of me, but my camera had frozen due to the cold. We then just shook hands and prepared for the long descent.

I remember thinking of Mo Antoine's quip in his book titled *Feeding the Rat* of, "When you reach the top you're only half way there, the descent when people relax is when most accidents occur." Was it a premonition?

While carefully retracing our path down the summit snow slope a Swiss jet fighter flew at the Matterhorn and pulled up in an almost vertical, supersonic climb directly above us. Amazingly the hotdog pilot repeated the run six times. The sound from the jet's duel engines were so deafening that it frightened the living daylights out of us. We actually stopped in our tracks and instinctively ducked each time the screaming jet buzzed the solitary Alp.

Later when I was slowly making my way down past the uppermost part of the fixed-rope I thought I heard an unfamiliar sound. Previously, and as expected the only noise was the jingle-jangle of my equipment, the wind, and a falling rock or two. Whatever it was it just floated by me on the wind, and I dismissed it as my imagination. When the faint and out of place sound drifted by me once again I just shook my head and laughed it off. I was thoroughly convinced it was the wind playing its usual tricks. Then I had to stop for just a moment to study a rather dicey move. I again heard the elfin-like sound, but this time I decided to remove my stocking hat, cock my head, and listen as intently as I could. Sure enough the peculiar sound rose up from below once again.

When I very slowly scanned the steep slope below my curious gaze locked on the terrified eyes of a young woman desperately clinging to the rock. She was weeping, and my first thought was that she must have been frightened like Herwig and I had been by the jet fighter.

Suddenly a few feet below her, a man clothed in a red parka came around the sharp corner of the ridge. He shouted up to me, "Go back up! A man has just fallen to his death!"

I was stunned. I hung on the rope temporarily paralyzed unable to move. A number of our group was still ascending the route somewhere below me, and I dreaded that it was one of them. From that point at the base of the fixed rope section you would fall 3,000 feet before coming to rest on the Frugg Glacier.

The mystery man in red reappeared and broke my paralysis by angrily announcing, "I'm a Swiss Patrolman! ... Go back up the rope!"

Still shaken and confused, I slowly began to re-ascend back up towards where Herwig had me on belay. Slack in the rope drooped at my waist and then hung at my feet. I knew Herwig could feel it and would be troubled by not knowing what the heck I was doing or why. When I popped up in his line of sight with an arm full of the slack rope he had an angry expression on his face, and while still holding his end of the rope with his brake hand, he started waving with his free arm for me to go back down.

When I continued to approach him, he angrily snapped, "What are you doing?"..."Go back down!" A shocked look of disbelief replaced his frown when I got close enough to him and almost tearfully blurted out that somebody had fallen. I then explained the instructions I was given by the patrolman.

The two of us sat mute at the exposed belay stance on the west side of the ridge, while the bitter cold wind rounding the corner battered us unmercifully. We waited fifteen minutes. Then when our teeth began to chatter as we shivered uncontrollably, we realized we had to move down.

I cautiously passed by the terrified woman and saw that the Swiss rescuer had thoroughly lashed her to the mountain. Her tearing eyes were as big as saucers when I approached her, and she was clinging to the rock with everything she had.

When Herwig and I both had arrived at the bottom of the fixed rope the patrolman informed us that he had radioed for a helicopter to evacuate her. Apparently the woman had been climbing with a man who fell. We asked the patrolman if there was anything we could do to help and he assured us that we should just continue to descend. It was a polite way of telling us he had his hands full and that we'd just be in his way.

After dropping down another 20 feet I saw a tiny red speck appear in the clouds below us. I couldn't hear it yet but quickly realized it was the chopper. It rose towards us at what seemed like a snails pace, and when it got closer I thought it resembled a giant-prehistoric dragonfly rising up out of the mists. When it neared our location my mind shifted back to reality as gusts of wind swung it back and forth, and several times its whirling rotor blades came perilously close to the rocky slopes. But its skillful pilot soon had the craft hovering directly above the woman.

Instead of continuing our descent we stood there transfixed by the drama playing out just above us. It was as if we had been hypnotized by the pendulum motion of the leather chest and waist harness clipped to the end of a cable being lowered from the big ship to the patrolman's grasp. After three near misses he deftly grabbed the swaying harness on its fourth pass and quickly had it strapped on the woman. He then unclipped her from the mountain, signaled the pilot by radio, and the chopper immediately shot away from the rock face. The poor woman was instantly suspended over about 8,000 feet of empty air and very slowly winched aboard as the ship headed back to Zermatt.

We returned to the task of getting ourselves safely off of the mountain. Still taken up by all the adrenaline, our belays of each other were tighter and we took each and every step downward with greater care as the easier lower slopes suddenly seemed more threatening. But then my mind began to wander aimlessly as the alertness began to wear off and fatigue began to slowly consume me.

The Matterhorn has an atrocious reputation for rock falls and we heard the occasional clatter and sometimes-sharp pinging report of falling rocks from above, and silence once again as they became airborne.

Our escape from the sober mood on the mountain came to a standstill as we encountered a traffic jam at the Solvay Hut, where several other parties were waiting their turn to rappel from the steel-pipe railing installed as a guardrail on its small cement platform.

It was nearing dusk when we finally reached the bronze Madonna and Child statue at the base of the climb. Jim Ebert and another party of three from our group scheduled to do the climb the next day with one of the Austrian Guides met us there. They had been outside the hut earlier and had witnessed a different chopper fly by with a body bag suspended on a cable beneath it. Like us, they hadn't known who had paid the ultimate price that day, and the spouse of one of the three climbers with Jim was still on the mountain in a rope team of four. She was in tears and I quickly assured her we'd met her husband on our way down below the accident site. I also told her that they had still been ascending the route.

Her relief was very short-lived because right then we heard the ominous, deep-throated crump, crump sound announcing that something really big was coming down the mountain. We all turned in unison, looked back up towards the East Ridge and stood there with our mouths a gap as a bus-sized block tumbled and caromed right down the route near where Herwig and I had so recently just descended.

A queasy, nauseous feeling filled the pit of my empty stomach. It was as if the Matterhorn gave us one, last-parting warning that day. That incident and the death of the climber earlier, extinguished any thoughts Jim had entertained of letting the party of three try and climb the mountain in the morning. I'm not sure any of them were really too disappointed.

When all of us were safe and back at the hut we eventually learned that the climber who had fallen was a young German. Nobody knew how or why he fell, but I figured he maybe had been startled by the jet or just lost his grip on the fixed-rope like I almost did that morning.

In the hut's common room that evening the other successful climbers in our group shared their stories of the day's climb with a number of climbers (two from as far away as Nepal) planning to climb in the morning. I just sat in a chair in a corner by myself with a half-liter of tea for company and kept visualizing the terrified eyes and frightened expression on the young woman's face as I slowly approached her. It was as if she was convinced I was the Devil come to throw her off of the mountain. Under the circumstances, my heart was full of sorrow for the woman and the family of the dead climber, and I just wanted to be back in the hotel in Zermatt with Judy.

Acknowledging congratulations from others for reaching the summit felt awkward. Before retiring I pondered my own mortality and what Judy, the rest of my family, and my

friends would suffer if it had been me who had fallen. It wasn't the first time or the last time I questioned why I climbed.

View of the Southwest Ridge of the Zinal Rothorn from the Riffelhorn summit. (Photo by author)

Bright and early the next morning Jim Ebert and I raced each other down to the Hotel Schwarzee to catch the first lift back down to Furi.

A farewell party was held that evening at the Hotel Garni Adonis for those in our group who had only come for three weeks. They were scheduled to leave for Munich in the morning. Three of our Austrian Guides also had to return home. The rest of us had two more days to enjoy in Zermatt before traveling to Chamonix, France. After exchanging addresses and bidding our farewells, those of us staying behind discussed additional climbing and hiking opportunities.

Hans Steyskal approached me and asked if I would be interested in joining him on a more challenging climb. He explained how he had always wanted to ascend the Southwest Ridge of the Zinal Rothorn (Red Fortress). With the emotional pain of the previous day still fresh on my mind and my leg muscles protesting the rapid descent from the Hörnli Hut, I declined his invitation.

The weather in the morning was perfect and a number of the climbers in our group chose to ascend the Riffelhorn -- a rock outcrop above Zermatt where the Swiss Guides take their prospective clients to see if they have two left feet before taking them up the Matterhorn or any of the other big peaks surrounding Zermatt. I tagged along with the group and soloed the easy climb.

While standing on the broad, flat summit of the Riffelhorn my gaze was pulled away from the spectacular view of the Matterhorn, like a nail attracted to a magnet, to the striking Southwest Ridge of the Zinal Rothorn.

After returning to Zermatt, Judy told me that Hans was waiting for me on the swing set in the backyard of our hotel. He couldn't get anybody else to accompany him on the climb and still harbored hopes that he could change my mind.

Naturally I was dead-tired. All I wanted at the moment was to soak in a tub, enjoy a couple of beers, and have a nice dinner with Judy.

But when Hans offered to wait, while I took that soaking bath and offered as an additional incentive to carry the rope and my plastic boots all the way up to the Rothorn Hut (The steep hike up the Trift Valley to the pleasant Rothorn Hut gains 1700 meters or about 5,300 feet in elevation over a distance of about eight miles), I surprised myself and acknowledged the hidden desire I felt every time I snuck a peak at the long ridge leading up to the summit of the formidable Alp and told him, "I'll be ready in a half-hour."

I took a quick soak in the tub, donned my tennis shoes instead of hiking boots, and the two of us left together at 5:30 p.m.

The next morning at precisely 6:00 we followed some other climbers in the dark, but soon learned that they were off to ascend the Ober Gabelhorn. We changed our course and mistakenly ascended up to a dead-end on top of the ridge located just to the west of the hut. We quickly reversed ourselves, returned back to the hut and found the correct start for our climb was directly behind it.

On the move again we ascended the glacier above the hut up to its

Bergshrund -- a generally large crevasse that forms at the head of a glacier when it detaches from the rock wall behind it. Once we overcame the vertical wall of firm snow at the back of the Shrund, we passed over a large gentle snow slope that led to the top of a relatively level outcrop. From there we descended east down to another glacier and traversed it all the way up to the base of the 300-foot slope of mud, ice, and loose rock that rises up to a small notch in the middle and on top of the Rothorn's southwest ridge.

After struggling up to the top of the narrow, serrated ridge we enjoyed the unparalleled 360-degree panorama of glacial moraine, glacial ice, the surrounding Alps and a dark-blue almost violet colored sky. Behind where we stood the view is dominated by the Pte du Mountet, and directly in front of the Ober Gabelhorn and slightly north of the Wellenkuppe, the Trifthorn. Beyond the Ober Gabelhorn, the black shark-like tooth of the Dent Blanche lacerates the skyline. And standing alone more to the south is the imposing North Face of the Matterhorn. To the west you can see all the way to the French Alps dividing the border between Italy and France with Mont Blanc in dominion. To the east of the Matterhorn is the raised barrier between Italy and Switzerland consisting of the Furgghorn, Theodulhorn, Klien Matterhorn, Breithorn, the two snow clumps of Pollux and Castor, Monte Rosa and finally the Dufourspitze. Across the Visptal Valley, Dom fills the view to the southeast above Täsch, the Mettelhorn stands directly to the east, and of course the elegant and almost perfect pyramid of the Weisshorn rises just to the northeast.

I thought at the time that if I ever came back to the area I wanted to climb the Weisshorn. Judy and I did return to Zermatt in September 1992, but besides taking long hikes our only ascent was the strenuous walk-up to the 11,197-foot summit of the Oberrothorn.

Despite the vantage point only a privileged few will ever enjoy, Hans and I quickly focused our attention on the sheer drop-offs to either side of us. The exposure is tremendous and increases to thousands of feet as you progress up the narrow ridge.

Hans lead the entire way. And while he probed around each and every gendarme on the ridge to determine which side to traverse, I began to notice time slipping away. We were three hours behind our planned schedule and nowhere near the vertical rock pitches leading to the summit.

Author ascending the Southwest Ridge of the Zinal Rothorn.
(Photo by Hans Steyskal)

The crucial pitch of the climb is at an elevation over 13,000 feet. It involves negotiating a difficult chimney on the north side of the Alp, and on that particular day portions of the inside of the chimney were coated with a thin layer of black ice.

Struggling up the slick marble hard icy sections in bulky plastic boots with a pack on my back and an ice axe tucked beneath it, after already negotiating 22 rock pitches and expending almost all of my reserve energy, took everything I had. Forget style, I squirmed up through the narrow chimney anyway I could. I used my knees, elbows, butt, everything but my teeth. I still almost came off when the top of my ice axe stuffed between my pack and my back caught on a protruding rock. But I was proud that I never weighted the rope.

Hans wore a broad smile when I reached him at the belay above the crux pitch. And, I noticed he removed two pieces of protection instead of just one that he customarily had used on all of the previous pitches for an anchor.

At that point we still had to negotiate five more high-angle pitches and one nearly level pitch leading up and over to the 13,849-foot high summit. The final vertical pitch was on the sheer north face and was protected by three pitons.

On the traverse of the last pitch leading us over to the summit, one, exhilarating, heart-stopping move exists just below the summit block where you have to negotiate a one-inch wide edge that just happens to be right beneath a large, protruding bulge in the rock that attempts to push you off, and there is only air beneath your bottom and the Hohlicht Glacier 2,550 feet below.

It was 4:00 in the afternoon when we topped out. Zermatt was 10,720 feet below us and at that moment it seemed like it was a hundred miles away. We took turns posing next to the six-foot high, bronze crucifix on the coffee table-sized summit for a photo. And just before leaving for home a glider silently passed beneath us and its pilot waved to us.

Author on Zinal Rothorn summit. (Photo by Hans Steyskal)

View to the south from Zinal Rothorn summit. Note small plane in upper right hand corner. (Photo by Hans Steyskal)

The descent was brutal. Another climber had fallen earlier in the day, while attempting to ascend the South Ridge. It's the normal route taken to ascend and descend the Zinal Rothorn from the Zermatt side. We had noticed a chopper circling low in that area, while we were ascending the upper section of the Southwest Ridge. It's not that unusual to see helicopters coming and going throughout the Zermatt area, and once the big bird descended out of our view we dismissed it and concentrated on the climb.

As we approached the particular knife-edge section of the South Ridge we could see where a small section of the snow pack on the west side of it had given way. At that point the ridge is significantly undercut and terribly exposed.

I leaned out as far as I dared to look below, but I couldn't see where the base of the ridge joined the glacier approximately 1,000 feet below. There was, however, very fresh rock debris further out on the glacier.

Hans had me on a very tight boot-axe belay as I used my ice axe and the front points of my crampons to gingerly traverse across the near vertical slope. It wasn't the first time I cursed myself for not having a second ice tool. I had to dig in the snow for purchase with the fingers of my left hand and every time I did or struck the snow with my axe and kicked a step I half-expected the snow to slide off the rock below it and leave me dangling in space. Not the best Catholic boy in the pew, I prayed to God and Mother Mary for my safety just like every other time I've felt my life threatened in the mountains. Time seemed to stand still until I actually stepped down onto the rather flat snowfield on the down side of the ridge.

Then while I belayed Hans over to me a party of four Frenchmen approached from below. They waited impatiently for Hans to come across the vertical slope. I noticed that they were watching us with some bemusement. Apparently not knowing what had happened to another climber on the same section of the route earlier that day and the lousy condition of the snow pack, they obviously thought we were just two overly cautious American climbers.

Hans informed them of the situation after he joined me, but they just smiled and began to saunter across the treacherous section un-roped as if they were taking a walk in the park.

It's little wonder why so many lives are lost in the Alps compared to the North American mountain ranges. It's clearly not just the greater numbers of Alpinists enjoying the Hills in Europe, but their cavalier attitude as well. I figure a good part of the reason for their lack of caution must be the many huts offering safe refuge in adverse weather conditions and the readily available helicopter rescues.

It was 8:00 p.m. when we walked through the door of the wonderful Rothorn Hut. Hans quickly ordered us dinner, and an hour later we prepared to continue our descent to Zermatt.

It would be my second epic descent in three days. The glacial-fed stream draining the valley we had so easily stepped across on flat stones on our way up to the Rothorn Hut a day earlier was boiling with additional melt-water. We spent a nervous half-hour tripping and stumbling over rocks and small boulders, while searching in the dark back upstream to find a shallow enough stretch to cross. Then we had to locate the trail again lower down, and white moths drawn to our headlamps were so numerous at times you'd have thought it was snowing.

When we finally hobbled on rubbery legs onto the lighted and deserted streets of Zermatt it was 12:45 a.m. I was never so thoroughly exhausted in my life. Unfortunately, we were scheduled to leave for Chamonix, France that very morning at 7:30.

We silently approached the hotel Hans was staying in and there were no lights on, but he was able to hoist himself up onto the second story deck and knock on the patio door to his room. One of the other guides he was staying with then let him in. My hotel was further up the street and there also were no lights on in it. I grabbed hold of the front door and it was locked. I didn't know what to do. I went around to the backyard and sat on a picnic table in the side yard to wait for sunrise.

A woman in our group opened her fourth floor window at 6:00 a.m. She leaned out and was checking out the new day when I yelled up to her. She quickly recognized me and understood my predicament, came downstairs, and let me in.

Judy never said a word as I took another quick bath before crawling into bed to get at least a couple of winks. When we got up I was told that Jim and others in our group were quite concerned since they had expected Hans and I to return the previous afternoon.

In Chamonix, my cold returned accompanied with a severe sore throat, and I ended up spending a day in bed. Feeling miserable I promised myself I'd relax for the rest of the outing and stay behind with the hikers. The way I saw it I had grabbed the golden ring and completed the most difficult ascent of the trip with Hans. Eighteen other climbers in our group ascended Mont Blanc. At 15,771 feet, it's the highest peak in Western Europe.

Before we departed for home those of us who had been able to stay on for the fourth week of the outing spent our last two nights in Munich in the Lowenbrau Beer Hall hoisting overflowing, 38-ounce steins of golden, foaming suds; enjoying the many fast and deep friendships we'd made; and recalling the events of the last four weeks.

IN A GUIDE'S BOOTS

Jim Ebert asked me to be a climbing leader for the 1991 Iowa Mountaineers Mount Assiniboine Mountaineering Camp. Stepping into the shoes of a guide in the Canadian wilderness turned out to be more demanding and stressful than my day job of overseeing Wisconsin's landfill siting process. In fact, I was fortunate to have returned home in one piece.

I drove to Jim's residence in Iowa City, Iowa, after work on July 25. John Preussner, another climbing leader and close friend of mine from Dundee, Iowa, was helping Jim pack group equipment, food, and other essentials into a U-Haul trailer when I arrived.

The three of us left Jim's place late that evening in his deluxe van with the packed trailer in tow for Devil's Tower National Monument, Wyoming, to pick up resident climbing guide, Andy Petefish. After Andy joined us we drove straight through to Banff in Alberta, Canada.

Our first priority after arriving in the famous tourist town was to soak our road-stiffened muscles in the soothing mineral waters of the Banff Hot Springs. The cave-like facility is a far cry from the lavish, outdoor pools in Radium Hot Springs in British Columbia, I had enjoyed after my first Iowa Mountaineer Outing to the Commander Glacier area in the Purcell's back in 1988.

Before heading to the Banff campgrounds we ate pizza at a packed joint named Earl's and drained two pitchers of Earl's White Albino Rhino Ale. Under John's protests we notified our waiter at Earl's that it was John's birthday. The waiter offered him a free pint if he would stand up on his chair. When John reluctantly complied, the waiter handed him the beer and loudly announced to the totally packed second floor that John was celebrating a birthday. The noisy conversation throughout the large, upstairs room immediately ceased and everybody joined in as the waiter belted out a rousing, out-of-tune rendition of Happy Birthday. A number of bawdy toasts followed from all of the other tables. Then John chugged his free beer.

The next morning we met the 18 outing participants at the heliport parking lot of the Canmore Municipal Airport. One of them was from

Norway, another was from Colorado, two came from Utah, a newly married couple hailed from Minnesota, and the rest were from either Iowa or Illinois. The majority of them had little or no previous climbing experience.

After introductions we weighed the group equipment and supplies. Then we sorted out 40 lbs. of personal gear for each participant and each of us, which was to be flown into our remote Base Camp with Jim and John by helicopter.

Andy and I then met everybody else the following morning at the Mount Shark Trailhead, which is located at the end of the 18.5-mile dirt road from Canmore that leads through the gap between Mount Rundle and Chinaman Peak to the southwest end of Spray Lakes Reservoir.

From the Trailhead it's a 16-mile hike on Bryant Creek Trail through a section of Banff National Park and over Assiniboine Pass to our assigned Base Camp at O'Brien Meadows.

Magog Lake -- at an elevation of 7,200 feet -- sits nearby at the northern foot of Mount Assiniboine and is the largest water body in the park. Mount Assiniboine is the highest peak in the Canadian Rockies south of the Township of Banff. From the east, the 11,867 foot high peak bears a striking resemblance to the Matterhorn. Just like its counterpart in Switzerland, the easiest route up the Canadian mountain also has a reputation for rock fall hazard.

A few drops began to fall as we began the long hike to O'Brien Meadows, which eventually turned into a light drizzle, then it poured, stopped, and drizzled on us again. Despite the soggy weather we made good time and covered the entire distance in seven hours.

The overcast sky began to clear just as we arrived at the big meadow, but the welcomed sunshine and a spectacular view of Mount Assiniboine came with a price. The rain had kept the bugs at bay, but as soon as it stopped we were attacked by swarms of mosquitoes. You could sit in your tent, take a bath in repellent, or cover yourself with heavy clothing. It was still 65 degrees but I chose the latter defense. It clouded over towards evening preventing the temperature from dropping low enough to discourage the miniature, winged vampires. In the morning while John and I were making oatmeal and coffee for the entire group several landed in the large pots of boiling water. Almost everybody commented about the floating grounds in the coffee and the weird looking raisins in the oatmeal. John and I just smiled and offered seconds.

Twelve of us set off after breakfast with as much gear and food as we could carry and ascended the Headwall above Magog Lake up to the Bob Hind Hut. The hut (a small Quonset-type shelter) is situated on an exposed, flat outcrop at an elevation of 8,500 feet near the base of the East Ridge of Mount Strom. The safest route up the 1,000-foot high headwall is called Gmoser's Highway. It begins well to the right of a prominent snow gully that splits the wall, and a visible climber's trail leads up through a scree-covered slope to sheer cliffs and a major ledge system. From there the route is indistinct.

We roped up into three parties of four below the first ledge and Andy led the way. He marked his route using wands -- thin bamboo poles with small bright orange flags attached.

While ascending the first snowfield a muffled gurgling revealed the presence of a hidden stream below it. The gentle melody seemed harmless enough, but Jim warned that a number of climbers have lost their lives in the past by falling through the snow cover on the large gully that sits directly below the Assiniboine Icefield, where the main meltwater channel feeding Lake Magog forms a large tunnel.

Everybody waited while Andy was belayed up to the next ledge, where he discovered a couple of rare solid placements to place pitons for an anchor. Andy fixed a rope and threw it down to the rest of us to help safeguard our passage over the smaller buried stream.

Above the fixed rope the so-called highway continues through a weakness in the rock that has been widened over time by the action of the running water. John christened it "The Gateway to Hell." The name fit the eroded gap, because its easy access up to the next higher ledge draws you in and it's a natural funnel for all of the rock fall from higher up. The hazard is quite extreme since the exposed rock of the entire Headwall consists of highly weathered limestone.

We escaped the gateway where it dead-ends by ascending its left side to where a two-foot wide ledge runs laterally for a long distance over a vertical drop of several hundred feet. Unfortunately, protection is non-existent. Keeping your balance on the narrow ledge with 70 lbs. on your back is a difficult feat and I wasted nervous energy every time someone attached to my rope tripped or dislodged a rock.

Eventually we encountered a small waterfall cascading down the adjacent rock wall that had cut through the ledge to form a shallow and short streambed before continuing its vertical flight down to Lake Magog. Crossing the trench of flowing water was treacherous as it contains several well rounded, polished and slime covered rocks. I wanted to untie from the rope I was leading because if anyone slipped and fell the entire rope team could easily be pulled off.

The narrow ledge finally ends at a steep snowfield that leads up to a number of easy switchbacks that zigzag up to a large boulder field. Once we picked our way through the scattered maze of house-sized rocks we encountered one last long, steep snowfield located just below the hut.

The stress involved and the energy expended to get to the hut were well rewarded by the incredible views. The massive, tumbling Assiniboine Ice Field and the nearby snow-capped Mount Magog are located just to the west. Directly to the south tan, black, red, and gray bands of limestone rise like so many stairs up the 6,000-foot high North Face of Mount Assiniboine. To the east, the vista stretches back down the upper snowfield to the rim of the Headwall. From there it abruptly plunges a 1,000 feet down to the deep blue azure waters of Magog Lake before expanding off to light green meadows, dark green forests and more distant gray snow-streaked peaks too numerous to count.

Jim, Andy, and John spent the night at the hut. The plan was for the three of them to reconnoiter the North Ridge on Assiniboine the following day and to fix rope on the hardest sections of it.

After dumping our loads the rest of us needed to return to Base Camp to fetch sleeping bags and additional provisions. I was concerned about rock fall, because the sun had the entire day to work on the ice holding loose rock on the Headwall. I begin to relax only after we reached the base of the cliffs and began crossing the wide, scree slope down to the Lake Magog shoreline.

My relief was erased when a sharp report that sounded like someone had fired a howitzer startled us. Fooled by the tremendous echo that bounced back from the valley below us we all looked down towards Base Camp. Then I sensed something was amiss and quickly spun around to look up. I was astonished to see a large section of the rock face directly above us just collapse and initially appear to fall in slow motion. But then the whole mass collided with the first ledge below it and exploded into cannonball-sized rocks that immediately gathered missile like speed.

There was absolutely nowhere to hide. I just screamed at

everybody, "Hit the dirt!" And for a couple of terrifying seconds I thought we were all dead men. But the rocks smashed into the scree slope just above us and unbelievably bounced right over us.

When the pungent smell of ozone created by the numerous rock splitting impacts and dust cleared I dreaded hearing cries or moans of pain. After again checking the headwall above us I asked, "Is everybody okay?" The others all timidity responded that they thought they were.

Only then, did the mixture of fear and relief at our surprising luck hit me. I couldn't believe we all survived unscathed. I wearily glanced upwards one final time before instructing everyone to leave our wanded route and hightail it straight down the rest of the scree slope. Shaken and giddy at the same time from having cheated the Grim Reaper we finished the descent at almost a run.

Physically drained and emotionally relieved when we reached our campsite I just wanted to collapse into my tent. Yet I still had to prepare dinner for my group and plan a hike for the rest of the outing participants who would be staying behind for another day.

In the morning three of the climbers that had endured the cannonade up on the scree slope decided to stay behind to do a walk up peak with one of the hiking groups. I was also less than thrilled about repeating the wanded route back up the Headwall, and below the scree slope I made an executive decision. I decided to bypass the route we used the previous morning and wanded my own alternate path up to the higher ledges.

We met Jim, Andy and John half way up the final snowfield. They had just come off of the North Ridge and looked like they had been through a war.

"The route is in terrible condition!" Jim said. "It's all iced over and we were dodging falling rocks all day long." He then stated, "It's way too dangerous for our club members... I'm calling the mountain off-limits...It just isn't worth the risk of somebody getting hurt."

I told him about the rock fall incident on my groups previous day's descent and that I had established what I felt was a safer route up to the gateway. I also mentioned that the folks left behind were getting antsy. He decided to return to Base Camp with John to organize and lead the less experienced group on some more walkup climbs.

Jim's decision to abandon Mount Assiniboine was disappointing for a number of the participants, who had dreamed about scaling the mountain for months. Jim left Andy in charge, but both of us had to put up with a lot of grousing. Fortunately, there were no mosquitoes at high camp to add to the morale problem. Everybody's spirits were soon somewhat restored by the beautiful surroundings and nature's dazzling displays.

During the daylight hours a steady stream of rock fall and small avalanches rained down Mount Assiniboine and, almost every afternoon, thunderstorms developed below us and dumped on Base Camp. While just before dusk pinkish-purple sunsets reflected off of the mirror-like surface of Lake Magog. And each night ghost-like northern lights shimmered above us and meteors shot across the star-filled sky. I even felt a slight twinge of guilt because I knew Jim and John and the rest of the group had to deal with the dampness and bugs down in Base Camp.

The morning after arriving back at the hut, both Andy and I left before sunrise by headlamp with two rope teams of three. Andy was determined that we complete a traverse of Mount Strom and possibly an ascent of the higher and more challenging Mount Sturdee -- a rugged satellite peak of Mount Assiniboine.

Although a brilliant orange rim of flame above the distant peaks in the east announced a clear dawn, fog shrouded us up on Mount Strom's knife-edged East Ridge. The cloud cover lifted just as we neared the peak's broad and flat 9,800-foot high summit enabling us to enjoy a spectacular view of the Bob Hind Hut, Mount Assiniboine, and the Assiniboine Glacier. Once we were on Mount Strom's actual summit we could also see Mount Sturdee's Northwest Face, the snowcapped Purcell Range to the west, the granite spires of the Bugaboos to the northwest, and all the way to the glistening Columbia Ice Fields to the north.

After a short rest that included lunch, we traversed back across the bare, windswept summit o its southeast end to study the approach to Mount Sturdee.

The Southwest Couloir, which has a slope of almost 70 degrees, is the normal route taken up to a large cliffy buttress that leads to Sturdee's 10,400-foot high summit. From our airy perch we could see that we'd have to descend to the Strom-Assiniboine Saddle and plunge step down a very steep and unstable slope of scree to an unnamed ice field partly covered by large patches of pink algae-streaked snow. From there we'd then have to ascend the ice field up to the Assiniboine-

Sturdee Col in order to gain access to the very steep couloir on the southeast side of the castle-like turreted peak.

Andy pointed out large rocks from the West Face of Mount Assiniboine that had ended their flight on the left side of ice field. A couple of large open crevasses were also readily visible and faint shadows betrayed others lurking beneath the fragile surface of covering snow.

View from Mt. Strom summit of Mt. Sturdee's Northwest Face.
(Photo by author)

Once we made our way down onto the ice field, the open crevasses varied in color from turquoise when in direct sunlight to emerald green when shaded by a passing cloud. They also seemed to beckon us with their toothy, icicle smiles to come on over and have a closer look. We smartly kept our distance, carefully probed before each step with our ice axes, and kept an eye out for any slight indentations in the snow.

The weather held until we began kick-stepping our way up to the Assiniboine-Sturdee Col. When we arrived on top of the Col, black threatening clouds were billowing up from the south. After a slight hesitation and wondering if we should just hightail it for high camp, Andy said, "Let's go for it."

The snow within the Southeast Couloir was peppered with rocks from Sturdee's friable east ridge that towers above it. Moving as quickly as possible, our progress up the 300-foot couloir was slowed near its top when were faced with an unexpected stretch of ice.

A 100-foot high buttress, where the couloir tops out, also has to be scaled and adds to the objective risks of the climb with loose rocks sitting on its every handhold and foothold waiting to be nudged off of their perch to pummel someone below. It reminded me of the rock climbing I had done the previous year in the Italian Dolomites. Andy found a single rock horn halfway up the rotten buttress solid enough to sling for protection.

We were greeted by thunder at the top of the buttress, where the final obstacle guarding the summit is a narrow 50-foot high chimney. Andy quickly set up a bombproof rappel station for a quick escape back down the buttress to the snow couloir, while I led the group up to the summit.

Our arrival on the high point of the peak coincided with the first close flash of lightening and, almost instantaneously, a swift moving storm pelted us with wind driven hail that changed to sleet and then to snow in a matter of minutes. The varied precipitation accompanied by frequent, blinding flashes of lightening and deafening thunder made our hurried retreat back down the narrow chimney a gripping experience.

Then upon returning to the top of the buttress below the chimney, Andy had two climbers rappel down to its base at a time. Each climber used a single strand of the doubled rope Andy had fixed to his excellent anchor that included three solid pitons. Andy and I were the last two to rappel, and by the time we finished it the storm had already moved across the ice-filled valley over to Mount Strom.

When we unclipped from the rope, Andy pulled it down, then turned to me and drawled, "That was a close call...when I stood up to rappel my ice axe began to hum...I thought for sure we were gonna be toasted."

We still had to descend the rest of the high-angled couloir and a 3,000-foot drop yawns off to the right at the foot of it. Twice we buried two "deaden" (large wedge-shaped aluminum belay devices, which you bury in snow at the right angle so that they will burrow deeper into it and thus hold the progress of a fall) to protect our descent.

We took the next day off and Jim and John arrived just after noon with more of the outing participants. The two of them then returned to Base Camp to lead those still left below on some more hikes.

Two of the participants were a mother and daughter team. They were both blondes and clearly not the hardcore outdoor types. The mother expected to be waited on and at one point I was convinced she was going to ask me to do her nails. Guiding for me as a profession lost a lot of its luster after having to deal with her and some of the others.

Andy and I spent the next two days leading rope teams up different routes on Mount Strom, Mount Magog and Wedgwood Peak. On August 5, Andy left with everybody that hadn't yet ascended Mount Magog and the newlyweds asked me to take them up Mount Sturdee.

As a guide, you have to be extra-cautious and constantly evaluate each person's ability to make sure no one gets over his or her technical proficiency or "margin of safety" on a climb. Stepping off backwards above a 2,000 foot precipice to rappel for the first time isn't the most natural thing for a person to do. Before agreeing to take the young couple, I asked them if they'd rappelled before. I told them, "If you're not comfortable making the rappel then I can't take you." They both absolutely assured me it wouldn't be a problem because they'd done previous rappels in rock climbing classes they had taken while visiting Grand Teton National Park.

The husband is tall and lanky and his fiery red-haired spouse is quite short. I put her behind me and I tried to kick steps all the way up to the Assiniboine-Sturdee Col to match her short legs. She complained I was going too fast and her spouse tied in directly behind her countered she was going to slow. And wouldn't you know it, we had to make a quick retreat off of Mount Sturdee's summit because of another approaching electrical storm.

I had the new bride rappel off the end of the buttress first and she did just fine. But when her husband's turn came, fearing both the approaching storm and the void beneath his boots, he froze. Then he momentarily lost his balance and accidentally nudged off a football-sized rock.

"Rock!" I screamed. It apparently just missed his bride because she shrieked from below loud and clear, "Tom you fucker!" I looked Tom in the eyes and said, "I guess the honeymoon's over."

I then decided the only way I was going to get him to commit to the rappel was to try to act like we had all day. It worked. Below the steep couloir and around the corner a great glissade down to the ice field helped us make it back to the hut without even getting wet.

The next morning, it was time to descend back to Base Camp. I wasn't looking forward to going back down the tricky headwall with a heavy pack, the next day's long hike out to the Mount Shark Trailhead or, for that matter, returning to civilization. But I couldn't wait to get a hot shower, eat some real food instead of freeze-dried, down a pitcher of Earl's White Albino Rhino Ale and, most of all, be relieved of the responsibility for being anybody else's teacher, cook, mother, and pal at least for awhile. My hat is off to any outdoor Guide.

Higher Altitudes in the Cordillera Real

In 1993, I traveled to Bolivia with Mike Caldwell, a Colorado Mountain School Guide; Mike's 14 year-old son and now world famous rock climber, Tommy; Sue Spencer, a fellow hydrogeologist from Snowbird, Utah; Paul Cornia, a computer programmer from Thornton, Colorado; and Alec Patterson, a lawyer from Atlanta, Georgia.

Our goal was to climb two peaks in the Cordillera Real (Royal Range). Before tackling Nevado Illimani, the highest peak in the range at 21,205 feet, we planned to ascend the nearly 20,000 foot high Huanya Potosi for a warm up.

The expedition provided me with my first high-altitude climbing experience and opportunity to visit the Third World. My expectations for unforgettable mountaineering and cultural experiences were realized, but acute mountain sickness exacerbated by food poisoning cost me the Huayna Potosi summit.

Our American flight left Miami on May 29th at midnight and arrived at the J. F. Kennedy International Airport at 7:00 the following morning. The airport is also called "El Alto" because its terminal and runway are located on the Altiplano (high plain) at an elevation of 13,300 feet. When we deplaned it was like taking one step from Miami near sea level up to almost the top of the Grand Teton in Wyoming.

As soon as our duffels and packs emerged after we entered the bunker-like terminal we were whisked through customs and herded like dazed llamas to our waiting taxis – two old beat up Chevy's from the late 50's.

We sped across the dusty, pot-holed highway leading away from the airport and saw our first glimpse of the Capitol City of La Paz, which was equally inspiring and discouraging. The earth drops away from the highway to reveal a nearly 3-mile wide canyon filled rim-to-rim with shabby, dirt floor shacks that eventually lead down to modern high rises in its center and fashionable suburbs located even lower in the canyon where the air is also a little richer. And off in the hazy distance the snow-capped, triple peak of Illimani towers above the city.

When we careened down into the center of the city of 1.5 million with our brakes and springs screeching, the smell of asbestos and diesel fumes filled the interior of the late model cabs. Traffic was almost at a standstill on the Prado (main thoroughfare of the city), which follows the Rio Choqueyapu down the canyon. Eventually we made our way onto a cobbled side street and rolled to a stop in front of our hotel.

After checking in and taking a short nap we all took a stroll back down to the main drag. Fortunately for our noses -- like a modern day sewer -- the river actually runs underneath the stone avenue.

For our first lunch we sampled the Bolivian version of fast food called Saltines (spicy meat and vegetable pies stuffed with chicken, olives, eggs, potatoes, onions, peas, carrots, and whatever else might have been on hand), and a cup of mate de coca or coca leaf tea. The tea is reported to assist in acclimatizing to the high altitude.

Later that afternoon on another side street we stumbled across a parade consisting of school children accompanied by small brass bands. The kids were dressed in bright costumes and each class represented another country or culture. Festivities continued all that evening and the narrow street above our hotel was crammed full of color and with drunken humanity. Most every man and woman was either already plastered or on the way there. We joined in and quickly found the local beers, Pacena and Cerveza, to our liking.

Before retiring for the evening I was almost electrocuted when I reached up to turn off the shower. In order to turn it on or off you have to pull a chain switch attached to a bare light socket and bulb hanging from the ceiling of he stall. While in bed I browsed my Lonely Planet Bolivia guidebook and discovered the Residentcial Rosario, located within walking distance just up the street was highly recommended and reportedly served the best English breakfast in the city.

The next morning I convinced Mike, with the help of my comrades, that we should check out of dump we were at and move up the street. Mike is fluent in Spanish and he was able to procure rooms at the Residentcial Rosario with two double beds and a decent shower for only 34 Bolivianos (approx. $8.00) a night. We were impressed with the cleanliness of the place and the breakfast was as good as advertised.

On Monday, May 31, we spent time at an artesans' market and passed through the unique witchcraft market where self-proclaimed witches tried to sell us herbs and remedies, charms to protect us from spirits, blessings for our expedition, and dried llama fetus's to bring us good luck. Mike actually bought a fetus and the witch instructed him to bury it beneath his residence. I still can see him trying to explain to the U.S. Customs folks back in Miami on our return home what he had in his bags and why he had it.

Later in the afternoon we supplemented our provisions for the mountains at a huge food market located below street level in what seemed like the first floor of an underground parking lot in the states. It was my first exposure to seeing half a cow or pig hanging suspended on a hook from the ceiling in the open air or laying on a elevated wood table and covered with flies. We did actually find some good produce and boxed pasta.

The following day Mike arranged for a visit to Tiahuanaco -- a famous Pre-Incan city/ceremonial center located near the southern shore of Lake Titicaca. The construction of the ancient city was under way around 700 AD and its thought to have once been inhabited by approximately 20,000 people. Severe drought apparently led to the culture's decline and it dispersed into oblivion around 1200 AD. The visit is a very worthwhile day trip even considering the mandatory 6-hour, teeth-chattering, bus ride over an extremely dusty washboard dirt road to get there and back. On our way there we stopped up on a higher plateau to stretch our legs and take in the awesome view of our first objective, Huayna Potosi.

When we returned to the Rosario, Mike made arrangements with one of Bolivia's foremost mountain guides, Senor Alfredo Martinez Delgado of the Club Andino Boliviano, for our transport to the isolated trailhead that leads to the long approach to the base of Huayna Potosi.

The mountain's imposing beauty and easy access have made it very popular with climbers, but since access to the trailhead is by jeep it allows little time to acclimatize and a climber can quickly develop acute mountain sickness or worse, high-altitude pulmonary or cerebral edema. Either edema can be fatal. The only cure is to get an afflicted climber to a lower elevation as soon as possible, and it's

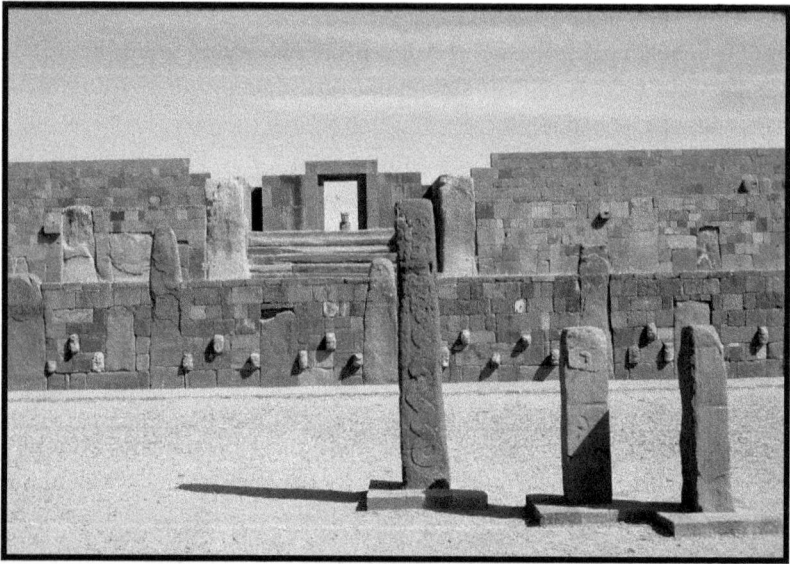

Tiahuanaco -- a famous Pre-Incan city/ceremonial center.
(Photo by author)

rather daunting to know that if you were to come down with either of the more serious illnesses there is no helicopter to come and rescue you. And even if you're able to get back down to La Paz, its elevation is too high to recover at and you would have to pay to be flown commercially to Santa Cruz, which is located down in the Amazon Basin.

On the way to the Huayna Potosi Trailhead you pass by the reservoir that serves as La Paz's drinking water source. The water is a beautiful turquoise color, except its upper end is stained yellowish-brown from toxic runoff seeping down out of tailings from numerous played-out tin mines located on the hillsides above it. You also pass by a cemetery for miners, where the glacier-draped 19,974 foot-high Huayna Potosi looms in the background. It's a haunting view, which not only reminded me of the miner's hardships and risks but of ours to come.

Normal route to ascend Huayna Potosi begins on the other
side of the reservoir. (Photo by Alec Patterson)

We were dropped off by a foot worn trail that starts from an
elevation of about 15,000 feet just three hours after leaving La Paz.
Initially the trail steeply descends to the cement dam holding back the
city's reservoir. After crossing over the top of the dam, the trail leads
across a winding and very narrow aqueduct that hugs an outcrop of
moss and lichen-covered black and white granite for a half mile.
Meltwater confined between the granitic wall and the manmade chute of
cement rushes by on its journey down to the reservoir. On the opposite
side of the elevated walkway there is a sheer drop-off of more than a
100 feet. While carrying 50 to 60 lb. loads we had to look at our feet at
all times. If we glanced down at the water running and moving within

the aqueduct in the opposite direction we were traveling we would get dizzy and begin to lose our balance.

After crossing the aqueduct, the trail abruptly turns left and leads straight up the narrow crest of a very long lateral moraine. Halfway up the moraine I began to feel lightheaded and to suffer a slight headache.

Mike finally stopped at approximately 16,000 feet below a large coal black buttress of schist and we established our first campsite. My head felt like it was going to explode every time I bent over to help set up one of our two tents.

After camp was established and with lots of daylight still left, Mike suggested we carry our technical climbing gear up another thousand feet and stash it to lighten our load for that section of the climb in the morning.

As we scrambled up through a steep gully choked full of unstable rocks, each step had to be taken with caution to avoid turning an ankle or a worse mishap. We had less and less oxygen to breathe as we gained elevation and my pulse began to race. When I started to get light headed I told Mike I couldn't continue. He asked the others to take my gear the rest of the way, while I waited for everybody to return.

In addition to my routine exercise regime, I had spent many weekends lugging a large, loaded pack up and down the steep quartzite steps on the bluffs at Devil's Lake State Park near Baraboo, Wisconsin. While it helped to increase my endurance and stamina, I knew that even former experience at such heights provides no assurance that you won't suffer from the debilitating effects of high altitude.

That night after dinner I became extremely nauseous, and while trying to sleep I had bouts of Cheyne-Stokes breathing (where like sleep apnea you miss a couple of breaths and then gasp for air). It was very windy and bitter cold and I was wearing every piece of clothing I had brought along. I was also zipped up tight in my mummy sleeping bag, and I panicked each time the nausea or irregular breathing would wake me. Then I would nod off, dream I was either strapped in a straitjacket or was suffocating and would wake up in a panic again. I had hallucinations and tiny veins in my eyes hemorrhaged. I later learned the eye problem is a common side affect of high altitude that indicates your brain is starving for oxygen. I hadn't realized the impact on my eyes until I had difficulty reading a restaurant menu after we had returned to La Paz.

Eventually during that miserable night I just lay awake and began to think about my family. I worried I was going to die thousands of miles away from home and never see then again. Finally I dozed off from total exhaustion just before dawn.

Because of my condition and the incessant rattle created by the tent fabric flapping in the brisk winds, both of my tent mates (Sue and Paul) also slept fitfully. Sue told me when we woke in the morning that she thought for sure they were going to have to carry me down off of the mountain in the middle of the night.

I felt better after eating breakfast and, as planned, we all prepared to proceed up to the normal high camp called Campo Argentino. It's located on a large glacial plateau at an elevation of approximately 18,700 feet.

The wind began to gust when we arrived and it was a major effort to set up the tents. Camping on a glacier also means dealing with the boring chore of melting snow in order to make meals and to fill water bottles. While squatting around the sputtering stoves waiting impatiently for the frozen lumps of white in our pots to transform into the liquid our bodies so desperately needed, one of our two dome tents ripped away from its moorings and begin to cartwheel down the glacier like an oversized beach ball. Before any of the rest of us could react, Tommy, the youngster in the group, sprang to his feet and tackled it just in time to save the day. We all gained a lot more respect for the wind and put a much greater effort into anchoring both tents.

Perfectly clear skies forecast a chilly night. Battened down and buttoned we slept with our plastic boots and water bottles in the bottom of our sleeping bags. When my wrist alarm went off at 3:30 the next morning, the wind was whistling outside and no one wanted to emerge from their warm cocoon of nylon and down feathers. The temperature minus wind chill was 25 degrees Fahrenheit below zero. Sue was the first brave soul in our tent to sit upright, squirm forward and fire up the stove under our tent's vestibule.

After chugging a steaming cup of hot chocolate and forcing down a bowl of lukewarm gruel, the three of us crawled out into the teeth of a 20-mph breeze. When it hit my face it felt like someone was scraping away my week old beard with a dull, pitted razor.

In good weather the normal route up the mountain is a pretty straightforward snow slog. The hardest section is ascending a fairly steep headwall. While approaching the headwall by headlamp, the surface of the glacier seemed alive. Waves of fine, windblown snow danced over its surface and the front of our cramponed boots. Up on the headwall the intensity of the wind grew and we became engulfed in a mad, whirling cloud of spindrift. Everything was a blur and we became totally disoriented. There was no up and no down. I almost didn't even see a gaping slot in the snow. It may have been a long scary ride before the rope came taut if I had gone in it. From that point on I hoped my partners skills at self-arrest wouldn't have to be tested.

On top of the headwall the unimpeded wind really hit us. We barely were able to stand up straight. It must have been gusting to at least 60-mph. The rope went limp and for a couple of minutes we all thought Mike had decided to turn back and was walking towards us. We couldn't see him even though he was only about 20 feet away. He later told us he was just trying to find the route.

Then five minutes later it was as if God had flicked a switch. The wind died so completely that our visibility went from near zero to more than 100 miles. La Paz and Illimani dominated our view to the north, the flat Altiplano stretched for miles and miles to the west and to the east we could see all the way to the humid and cloudy Yungas (highlands) that eventually descend to the lowland jungle of the Amazon Basin.

Up to that point my instincts kept telling me to bag it. But when our struggle against the cold and wind apparently was behind us, I became optimistic for the first time that morning.

At about 19,000 feet, however, I begin to stagger like a drunken sailor. No matter how hard I tried to establish a rhythm I could no longer keep up with the pace Mike was setting. Each time I strayed off of the well-packed route one of my legs would sink up to my hip in the adjacent, loose snow and I'd topple over. Fastened to the rope just ahead of me, Tommy would get jerked backwards every time I fell. I became embarrassed and my desire to continue evaporated faster than my sweat.

Mike called for a rest just below the Diretissimo Sur (Direct South Face), which is an 800-foot long, 50-degree snow slope leading up to the true summit. He guessed we were at around 19,200 feet and asked how we were all doing. I told him I didn't think I could or should go any further. But not wanting anybody else to give up their bid for the summit I suggested that I bivouac (fortunately, I had brought along a

Gore-Tex bivy sack) and wait for the rest of the group to ascend to the top and return. Mike checked me out to make sure I didn't have any serious symptoms of altitude sickness and agreed with the plan. He also had everybody else leave their packs with me to quicken their pace.

My ego was pretty bruised as I watched them leave, zigzag up the south face and eventually gain the impressive knife-edged summit ridge.

The next morning while doing the dirty deed on the open glacier, I learned I had a bug that almost certainly increased my susceptibility to acute mountain sickness. I had tried so hard to follow the medical advice "Boil it, peel it, cook it, or forget it." I also made double sure all of the water I drank and brushed my teeth with was either bottled or treated with Iodine, and I always kept my mouth shut tight when taking a shower. My downfall must have come from eating a piece of what looked like half of a "road-kill" chicken on top of spaghetti the night before we left for the mountain. We were in an Italian restaurant owned and run by a German old enough to have been in World War II.

I suffered a miserable descent that Saturday. While still crossing the glacial plain and tied in between Alec and Sue, it was interesting how quickly I was able to toss aside my modesty when I had to drop my pants.

We finally arrived back at our hotel in the late afternoon and I felt better in the heavier air almost immediately. I quickly gulped down a strong antibiotic for the bug, Lomotil to plug up my plumbing, and Diamox (a diuretic that helps one avoid getting altitude sickness in the first place). I then went to bed.

Everybody else of course was in the mood to celebrate their success and were disappointed when Alfredo told them that Bolivia's presidential election was scheduled for that Sunday, June 6, and that no alcohol's allowed to be sold for four days prior to the election. He also warned them that driving on Election Day or straying more than four blocks from your residence is strictly forbidden to avoid ballot stuffing.

We all took a long walk through the city early Sunday morning anyway. The streets were totally deserted except for a few small children taking advantage of the rare opportunity to play soccer in the empty streets. It was also a pleasant experience for us to not have to shout above blaring horns, try not to breathe in clouds of inky-black diesel fumes, constantly dodge other pedestrians, and be aware for speeding traffic. We did spend the entire evening at the hotel, however, and patted ourselves on the back for doing so after hearing what may have been several gunshots. Then again, it was more likely just firecrackers.

After two days of taking my medications, resting and relaxing, and also eating everything in sight I felt well enough to attempt climbing Illimani.

Mike had made arrangements with Alfredo to get us a ride to the Quechua Indian village of Estancia Una. To reach the remote village we traveled by jeep for four hours through an immense, scenic canyon on a one-track dirt road with lots of blind curves above thousand-foot drops. Our driver sped around each and every one of those curves tooting his horn and, after one close call of almost colliding with a huge black bull that ran across the road right in front of us, he proudly told us that he's the only one willing to make the drive. It was surely more dangerous then our climb to come.

Curious, dirty-faced children instantly surrounded us when we arrived in Una. While the rest of us took advantage of the photo opportunity, Mike made arrangements to have our larger packs carried to a Base Camp by horseback -- a distance of 10 tough, uphill miles. The horses had to be blindfolded before they'd accept our heavy backpacks on their backs. One bucked them off twice anyway. Finally when they were all loaded, we hiked behind them past scattered Quechua family huts that consisted of mud walls and grass roofs up to an uninhabited, high valley generally only visited by llamas, condors, local shepherds and their sheep.

I was really discouraged when I staggered into Base Camp dead last, and my confidence was further shaken when I looked up at the summit of Illimani still towering over a mile above it. It took three cups of coca leaf tea and two hearty servings of tortellini to revive me.

Quechua Indians loading our packs on horses in Estancia Una.
(Photo by author)

Alfredo had told us it takes six to eight hours to reach the high camp, which is located at 18,370 feet on a very small, snowy plateau perched above two enormous ice falls.

Mike had made a smart move by having hired porters to come up the next morning to haul the bigger packs up to El Nido de Condores or "Nest of the Condors," which is the normal Illimani high camp. With their help we made the ascent in five hours and by the time we finished chopping and shoveling out tent platforms, building a protective snow wall for the tents, and blowing up our sleeping pads we were all pretty exhausted.

It stormed most of that night but thanks to the antibiotics and Diamox, I slept and snored right through it. When I awoke at 3:00 in the morning I was surprised to find our tent's vestibule filled with snow. I got up and started one of our two stoves. Ironically both Sue and Paul seemed to be a little jealous that I had slept so well and was anticipating the backbreaking task ahead.

We began our ascent at 5 a.m. It was dead calm and so cold we couldn't feel our hands and feet. After proceeding by headlamp up a narrow ridge for two hours that started directly out of the high camp we encountered 35 to 40 degree snow slopes.

I started to feel fatigued and forced myself to take 10 steps before taking a rest, while we slowly zigzagged up the endless slopes. Thankfully, Alec had a crampon come off three times because I relished each of the unscheduled stops, while he muttered to himself and readjusted and tightened the errant spikes.

Above the snow slopes we had to skirt a large, menacing serac and leap over some crevasses that are reported to be as deep as 300 feet. The trickiest obstacle we had to overcome was a wall of smooth, marble-hard ice angled at about 60 degrees at an elevation of almost 20,000 feet. The totally exposed drop just to the left is over 4,000 feet. Mike carefully front-pointed up it, slammed in a picket for protection, and belayed us up one by one. Purchasing a tenuous hold with just one ice axe and standing on my front-points, I looked down only once. I then took a deep breath and made it a point not to again.

Finally at the top of the wall we were able to move into sunshine for the first time that morning, and all twenty digits of our hands and feet came back to life. The energy from the bright sun had also warmed the virgin snow, and it clung to our crampons as if it was mud. We all became taller with each step and had to constantly stop to knock the packed fluff off one foot with our ice axe while balancing on the other. I kept mentally going through the drill of what to do to self-arrest should one of us take a tumble.

Above the 21,000-foot level we were reduced to taking about four steps before having to lean on our axes and pant like winded dogs, and I began to question my sanity. I honestly don't know what kept me going, especially after like on the Matterhorn we encountered one after another demoralizing false summit.

Eventually it took an extraordinary effort to make your feet move one step upward. Then suddenly we heard a whoop from above. We all looked up and wondered why Mike was waving to us from what looked like just another ridge top. He told us to drop our packs, and one by one we joined him on the five-foot wide summit ridge to clasp his extended hand of congratulations.

We stood 885 feet above the height of Mt. McKinley (Denali), the highest mountain in North America, and peered down the sheer East Face, which plunges 5,000 vertical feet straight down from the summit. Mike quickly suggested we all just sit down. We then passed our cameras down to Paul, who was on the end of the rope, to shoot the mandatory group photo. I looked at my watch. It was 1 p.m.

I absorbed and tried to memorize the far view of La Paz, the rest of the Cordillera Real marching off to the south, and the magnificent but slightly lower south summit of Illimani. A couple of large isolated peaks to the north across the border in Peru also momentarily held my gaze.

After about a half hour, it was time to concentrate on getting safely back down, and Mike reminded us that we needed to summon what was left of our physical strength and mental capacity to stay alert. Back at the 20,000-foot

South Summit of Nevado Illimani. (Photo by author)

level we had to rappel down the steep ice wall. And further down the mountain where we could easily get distracted by the constant view, Mike pointed out that a number of climbers have fallen to their deaths while descending the snowy ridgeline above El Nido. His comments and concern got through to us. We all increased our efforts to keep the rope tight between us, and to make each and every downward footfall precise.

The clear weather held and we waltzed into high camp at 5:00 that afternoon. After a quick meal we collapsed in our bags completely spent before it even got dark.

When I ventured outside much later to take a leak, it was completely still. I looked up and the entire black dome above was ablaze with unfamiliar stars. The only formation I recognized was the Southern Cross. Standing there in the cold I again thought about why I climb. Like most climbers I usually don't have a good answer to the question when asked. It's certainly not just for the remarkable and incredibly beautiful summit views. I decided it's mostly because of the deep sense of accomplishment you feel after pushing yourself to your limits and the rare trust that is fostered and developed by the fellowship of the rope -- where you hold each other's lives in your hands. I've shared so many special moments of camaraderie with quite a number of other climbers, including some very interesting characters. Satisfied with my answer, I swallowed some more antibiotics and crawled back into the tent.

The next day we descended all the way back to Una in one push. We encountered a Swiss team halfway down to our former Base Camp. In four days they were the only other climbers we saw on the mountain, and Mike advised them of where he had left behind the picket we rappelled from.   On easier ground, I descended at too fast of a pace, well out ahead of most of the others and eventually developed blisters the size of quarters on my big toes. From then on each and every step was excruciating painful after they had popped. But knowing Mike had ordered a case of Grande Cervacas to be waiting for us kept my spirits up.

Under the influence of the drugs, alcohol, and fatigue the long ride back to La Paz seemed shorter and tamer then the ride up. I actually slept most of the way. But I distinctly remember our driver not using his headlights when it got dark and wondering why he had his radio on if he was trying to conserve his battery. Only in South America!

All of the hard work, physical discomforts, poor food, lack of appetite on the mountain, and lack of privacy and cleanliness soon faded in memory after the first hot shower, good restaurant meal, and night in a real bed.

From the left: Sue Spenser, the author, Alec Patterson, Tommy and Jim Caldwell pose on the higher North Summit of Nevado Illimani.
(Photo by Paul Cornia)

The following morning we were awakened by a brass band. I leaned out the third story window of the room Alec and I shared to see what was going on and saw a brightly dressed crowd of Bolivians with white confetti in their coal, black hair celebrating a wedding outside the small church next door.

Soon we were all leaning out of our windows watching a woman pour ChiCha (a yellow-colored, industrial strength maize liquor) from a pitcher into small glasses held out by several of the men in the crowd. They chugged it, grimaced and staggered, and then quickly held out their juice-size glass for another belt. According to my Lonely Planet Bolivia guidebook -- "There are several rumors concerning how ChiCha is made and if you are going to drink it you don't want to know."

On Friday, June 11, our last full day in Bolivia, Mike arranged for a taxi to take us to Copacabana. The small Bolivian resort on the shores of Lake Titicaca has served as a site of religious pilgrimage for centuries beginning with the Incas. Christianity was eventually adopted in the area, and in 1580 a direct descendent of the Inca Emperor carved the La Virgen Morena del Lago (Dark Virgin of the Lake). A number of miracles we reported to have occurred in the town shortly afterwards. The black, wooden statue now rests in a side chapel within a magnificent, Hispano-Moorish Cathedral that dominates the town's square.

After touring the gleaming white Cathedral we climbed Cerro Calvario -- a steep-sided hill that rises above the town where you can climb past the Stations of the Cross up to a small chapel. We then descended to Lake Titicaca. The lake is known as the highest navigable body of water in the world. The emerald green waters straddle the Peru-Bolivia border at an elevation of approximately 12,464 feet, and have a surface area of 5,400 square miles with a maximum depth of 1,532 feet.

We celebrated our successful trip on the outside patio at a small restaurant in Copacabana, where we consumed two bottles of wine with a delicious, Lake Titicaca trout dinner. It was a fitting and happy ending to our shared adventure.

MEXICAN TRILOGY

Dennis Domsie, an administrator at Iowa University in Iowa City, Iowa, walked up to me at Gate 12 in the United Terminal at Chicago's O'Hare Airport on Friday, January 14, 1994 and said, "You look like a Mountaineer". Domsie was on the same flight as me and, like me, was part of a team meeting in Mexico City. Later that same afternoon in the dark lobby of the Hotel Fleming after almost expiring on the capital city's smog, the two of us met Steve Broadie, a lawyer from Chicago, and Marko Cornacchione, our Colorado Mountain School Guide. Marko, who originally hails from the East, but had been residing in Fort Collins, Colorado, arrived in Mexico a couple of weeks earlier to guide another group, whose goal had been the same as ours -- to climb the Mexican Trilogy of high volcanoes or the 3rd, 5th, and 7th highest mountains in North America. Our final teammate, Steve Hunts, a budding photographer from Champaign, Illinois, arrived on a later flight.

While dining that evening at the hotel, Marko reminded us to all stay well hydrated to help us acclimatize to Mexico City's 7,340-foot high altitude. I had brought three liters of safe water from home just for that purpose, which now would be impossible ever since 9/11.

After dinner Marko introduced us to Miguel Najera and Cristobal Corovar. Miguel had been working with the Colorado Mountain School for several years and he took us to Garibaldi Square, where the pure and liquid notes of Mariachi trumpets floated on the quiet evening air. We purchased a lively song from one of the many silver-spangled, big sombreroed, uniformed bands before returning to our hotel t o rest up for the next day's itinerary.

Miguel met us early the next morning and took us on a whirlwind tour of the big foul-aired city. "Miguel is 72, but he walks like he's 20," Marko warned. Miguel had been feeling poorly that day but he lived up to his reputation. We were scrambling all day to stay with him on the city's crowded streets and subway tunnels.

First, he took us for a quick stroll by Chapultepec Park, which is to Mexico City what Central Park is to New York City. Across from the Church of Saint Francis, which was constructed in 1524, Miguel had us each read out loud a page about the historical church from his English guidebook. The recently restored church stands on the bed of the former Lake Texcoco and, now like the leaning Tower of Pisa in Italy, has a noticeable tilt due to subsidence of the unstable lake deposits beneath its foundation.

Miguel next took us to the main Post Office to mail some postcards. The ornate and impressive building was built in 1907, almost entirely out of marble imported from Italy.

We then walked to a nearby restaurant and grabbed a quick bite before riding the city's modern subway to the Zocalo (main plaza) to view the Cathedral, the National Palace, and the new "Templo Mayor" excavations. Miguel gave us his guided tour and interpretation of the excavations, which reveal part of the ancient City of Tenochtitlan. We also went through the adjacent, modern anthropology museum.

Near the end of the day we picked up some snack items at a SuperMarcado. The grocery store has 60 checkouts and is so large that the stock boys wear roller skates.

When we had finished our shopping we rode a small bus to Miguel's house where his wife, Aquilina, served us a delicious home-cooked dinner and maple nut ice cream for dessert. We all left the Najera's dinner table stuffed and slowly ascended the two flights of very narrow and steep steps to our sleeping quarters.

None of us were able to or ready to fall asleep, and the chemistry of our group was soon bonded by laughter. Steve Hunts repertoire of jokes virtually kept the rest of us almost in tears from laughing. We nicknamed him the "Joke Meister," and from that night on, it was his job to end each evening with at least one good joke.

What little sleep we did get at Miguel's was disrupted by staying too hydrated and having to make several perilous trips to the bathroom located at the bottom of the steep stairs. We were also awakened several times by an incessantly barking dog. We all plotted the dog's death many times over.

Aquilina served us a hearty Sunday morning breakfast before we loaded our gear into Cristobal's van to travel to Amecameca. The vile dog from the night before watched us in total silence through the fence on top of the flat rooftop from across the street.

When we arrived in the village of Amecameca, which on that day was dominated by a large and colorful market in its square, Marko instructed us to split up after giving each of us an assignment to purchase some fresh fruit and a few other necessary provisions. When we returned with our bounty we proceeded up the steep, windy road that passes through a large pine forest preserve, travels over the Paso de Cortes (the Cortez pass) to Tlamacas, and onto the Vicente Guerrero Lodge. The impressive and modern looking stone lodge is located within Popo-Izta National Park at an elevation of nearly 13,000 feet.

Popocatepetl rises to an elevation of 17,887 feet and literally looms above the lodge. The active volcano is almost a perfect cone of loose, black ash with a New York Vanilla-colored topping of dirty snow and ice.

A large volume of steam was spewing out of Popo's elliptical crater when we arrived, but the last time the volcano had really erupted was in 1540. It also had historical smaller eruptions through 1947. Then on December 12, 1994, the volcano erupted, and the following year a number of climbers were killed on its slopes when it suddenly began to belch out large volumes of gas and pyroclastics. The volcano has had many small eruptions since and had thrown lava almost 1,000 feet into the night sky during the early evening of December 18, 2000. That was the volcano's biggest eruption in 1200 years, and thousands living in its vicinity were evacuated. Even more recently, it erupted throughout much of 2013, and thin layers of ash repeatedly fell on several towns in the central state of Puebla, just 35 miles east of Mexico City. The huge capital city so far has been spared, even though one massive explosion threw ash and incandescent rock almost 2.5 miles skyward.

During our visit the mountain still had a reputation of being an easy walkup peak, with altitude being the only difficulty. But four climbers died on its slopes just the week before. Two Germans fell when their Mexican-made crampons broke; one Austrian slipped and fell while trying to traverse from a more difficult route to the standard route; and an American's chute collapsed when he tried to parapente from the summit.

I wasn't surprised when I heard about the parapenter's death. The winds around the volcano and the nearby extinct volcano, Iztaccihuatl (17,343 ft. high), are extremely unpredictable. Both volcanoes rise nearly two vertical miles above the surrounding countryside and steam boiling out of Popo's crater only added to the turbulence in the air around its slopes.

That Sunday afternoon there were literally hundreds of people visiting the lodge, hiking the many trails around Popo's lower slopes, or just having a picnic. There was trash everywhere!

The crowds virtually disappeared before nightfall and for the next five days; our companions primarily included a climbing group from Prescott, Arizona, some Canadian and Scottish climbers, and the lodge's staff.

That evening the lodge staff were watching the local news channel on a small television and we saw the devastation from the earthquake in San Francisco.

Marko prepared spaghetti for the evening meal, but despite Marko's warnings, Steve Hunts insisted on boiling and eating some potatoes he had purchased for himself at the market in Amecameca. On Monday, we did an acclimatization hike up to 14,500 feet and picked up five bags of trash on our way back to the lodge, and that night, just as Marko had predicted, Steve Hunts came down with the dreaded "revenge". Except for Hunts and Cristobal, the rest of us planned to leave for Popo's summit at 2:00 on Tuesday morning, but the only climbing Hunts was going to be doing for the next couple of days was out of his bunk bed to get to the porcelain throne. Cristobal was already so well acclimatized from the previous week's ascents that he planned to get a later start and catch up to us.

Although we had to travel by headlamp for almost five hours, the early Alpine start ensured there would be plenty of daylight for our return to the lodge. It also provided us the opportunity to enjoy an indescribably, beautiful sunrise with crystal-clear views of Izta before the mountain was smothered by clouds.

Ascending the loose ash slopes up Popo can only be described as sadistic torture. Imagine trying to scale a 3,500-foot high, black sand dune. We lost a step for every three we gained. Additionally, gas emanating from numerous vents made our eyes burn and water.

When we finally reached what we assumed was the snowline we were surprised it was instead a frozen, glittering sheet of rotten ice. It was quite sobering to know that in the case of a fall, any attempt to self-arrest with an ice axe would be futile.

Cristobal caught up with us just before we roped up, and I thought we would be off to the races. But the combination of the altitude, gas, a sinus infection, and inexperience walking in crampons slowed Steve Broadie's progress to a crawl. He eventually lost his voice and became so fatigued I thought we'd never make it to the crater's rim. Still, his doggedness determination impressed me, and when I was ready to call it quits my ego wouldn't let me as long as he kept methodically moving one shaky step at a time upward.

The altitude really began to impact me at about the 16,000-foot level. It was as if I ran into the preverbal wall. My legs felt like lead weights, and pain and exhaustion soon accompanied each cramponed step upward. My mind began to anticipate every little rest as if it were the only thing that mattered in the entire world.

Meanwhile, Marko kept turning around and inquiring, "How's everybody doing?" Every single time, Dennis Domsie would reply, "Fantastic!" I nicknamed him, "Mr. Enthusiasm". Dennis had wisely taken the drug for altitude called Diamox. Struggling just get a breath I tired of his enthusiastic replies and secretly vowed that if he shouted, "Fantastic!" one more time I was going to turn around and plant my ice axe in his helmeted noggin.

Later, when I was no longer suffering and thinking more clearly I admired his positive attitude. And, the two of us actually became close friends when the tables were turned while we were climbing Popo's neighbor, Izta. I actually had to encourage him not to give up when he suddenly experienced painful back spasms.

When we all ceremoniously stepped up onto the rim of Popo's crater, Steve Broadie collapsed as if he had been decked by an Evander Holyfield right cross. I thought he looked out for the count for sure and wondered just how on earth we were going to get him back down alive.

I felt rather lousy myself from the combination of the sulfuric gas fumes rising up out of the crater and the low oxygen at that altitude. When Marko asked Cristobal to take Broadie down, I volunteered to join them. Marko tried to discourage me at first, but then handed me his hammer, four pickets, and pointed out an escape route that avoided the ice sheet entirely. Then he and Steve Domsie left for the true summit -- a high point on the other side of the crater's rim that rises up another 800 feet.

Clouds had developed below us shortly after sunrise and had chased us all the way up to the crater. Leading the way, I became disoriented in the poor visibility but Cristobal cried out the couple of times I started to veer off in the wrong direction.

Behind me Steve was mechanically plunging down the soft slope on tired knees that began to buckle rather than support. I was just going to warn him to watch out for a large, unstable rock in his path, when he suddenly fell and slid for several feet. While struggling to regain his feet he inadvertently knocked the rock loose and it rolled right toward me. I danced out of harms way just in time, but by doing so twisted my right knee.

Broadie was barely able to walk and now I was limping along side of him using one of Marko's pickets and my ice axe for support.

Cristobal was in a big hurry, because he was leaving his van for us and needed to hitch a ride back to Mexico City. When we reached the more level Las Cruces hiking trail lower down the slope and Cristobal knew we were no longer in danger of getting lost he tied Steve's pack on top of his own and raced down to the lodge.

Still high on the volcano, our painful descent seemed to last forever. It was the first time I questioned why I ever wanted to climb a mountain and I swore to myself I'd never climb another. The two of us hobbled into the lodge at 4:30 that afternoon, and just two hours later -- Mr. Enthusiasm and Marko arrived back from the summit.

Marko drove us down to Amecameca in the morning and treated all of us to a great pancake breakfast. We also purchased a shower and I soon forgot about the misery on Popo.

That evening, Marko, Dennis and I prepared to climb Izta the next morning. The two Steve's both decided to stay behind in Tlamacus to try and recuperate before our attempted ascend of higher Orizaba. We all went to bed early that night, but I only caught snatches of sleep before my wrist alarm went off at 12:45 a.m.

Iztaccihuatl is known as "The Sleeping Lady" according to Aztec mythology. If you view the volcano from the west and use a little imagination it's easy to understand why. Its features are known as the feet, knees, belly, breast (summit), neck, head and hair.

The standard route to the Lady's breast is a long 12-mile round trip at high altitude. It begins below her feet at La Joya (ele. 13,124 ft). You pass over many false summits, and never even see the true summit until you're on top of the last false one. And then you're instantly demoralized when you spot it, because the true summit is only ten feet higher and still two miles away across a flat glacial expanse.

The jostling ride over huge potholes in the dirt road to La Joya felt like we were rafting rapids, except we weren't getting wet. Marko was at the helm and he dropped us off in the dark at 2:50 a.m. Then he backtracked a half-mile to park Cristobal's van near a radio tower station, because the isolated Trailhead has a reputation for being frequented by thieves.

Huffing up the steep trail leading to the small saddle near the Lady's feet I occasionally turned off my headlamp to gaze at the stars. They blazed with a constant light unlike those that twinkle above the polluted air of Mexico City.

When we topped out on the small saddle, the lights of Amecameca to our west and the city of Puebla to our east sparkled below us like so many jewels spread across the floor of a dark cavern.

We arrived at the Esperanza Lopez Mateos Hut, a small sheet metal shelter situated at an elevation of 15,908 feet, just as the eastern skyline burst into a brilliant orange. Adding to the striking sunrise was an impressive view of Popo. Its plume of steam cut horizontally across the blazing sky to well beyond our final objective -- El Pico de Orizaba (elevation 18,850 feet) located 60 miles off in the distance.

No longer Mr. Enthusiasm as I mentioned previously, Dennis developed back spasms. All of a sudden he just wanted to sit down and enjoy the dramatic scenery. Marko and I plotted to keep him putting one foot ahead of the other.

Popocatepetl crater steams in the background, while two Canadians traverse the La Arista del Sol (The ridge of the Sun) on Iztaccihuatl.
(Photo by author)

It was 11:30 a.m. when we reached the snowline and began to walk across the wide, snow-covered glacier towards the La Arista del Sol ("The ridge of the Sun"). I had to silently chant, "One, two, step," to keep up with Marko's pace. Dennis was struggling even more on the other end of the rope in the rear. Thin, playful clouds fortunately began to roll in behind us and provided us some relief from the intense heat of the high-altitude sun. Anticipating whiteout conditions we placed wands on top of the windswept glacier to guide our way back.

We stood on the anticlimactic summit at 1:30 that afternoon. Dennis continued to barely move on the descent, and it was apparent that darkness was going to overtake us before we returned to the Trailhead.

Once we were past a very confusing spot on the Lady's knees, where Dennis and I might easily take a wrong path leading down the other side of the volcano, Marko pulled me aside and said, "Paul, you shouldn't have a problem getting back from here...I'll race ahead to fetch the van to save us some time."

Dennis and I still found the last 1,500 feet of the descent a bit harrowing. There's also one other spot where the correct trail snakes around some small towers of remnant lava up on the top of the Knees, and other trails from the wrong side of the mountain intersect with the route at that point. Marko had specifically instructed me to remember to stay to the right after passing the weird towers, but fatigue was taking it's toll and I began to question whether I did, especially when darkness overcame us and we begin to hear the bawling of some cows. There had been no bovines in sight on the mountain's lower slopes that morning.

Just when I was convinced we had gone the wrong way I stepped down a short drop in the path stumbled and fell down. I quickly got up, knelt down, and inspected the high step with my headlamp. I was instantly relieved because I clearly recognized it as the very same high, loose dirt step we had struggled to climb up early that morning.

I was feeling quite punch-drunk after being on the move for over 17 hours at altitude when Marko met us with the van at 8:30 p.m.

When we returned to the Vicente Guerrero Lodge, the two Steve's were so concerned that they apparently were just about to request a search and rescue.

The following morning, Cristobal and Miguel met us down in Amecameca. After another breakfast of pancakes, Miguel returned to Mexico City by bus and Cristobal drove the four of us to Joaquin

Canchola's residence in Tlachichuca.

Joaquin's wife, Guadalupe, and his beautiful daughter, Mary Beth, served us another great home-cooked meal that evening. The family also put us up for the night. I was embarrassed when Guadalupe insisted I place my sleeping bag on Mary Beth's bed. She apparently shared her parent's bedroom.

In the morning, Joaquin gave us and another group of climbers from Arizona a ride up to the Octavio Alverez Hut, a rustic stone building located at Piedra Grande (elevation 14,500 feet) on the North Slope of Orizaba.

The one lane, steep and winding dirt track to the hut is extremely dusty when dry and muddy and impassable when wet. The ride in the open back of Joaquin's tandem-wheeled truck was quite an experience. We had to hang on to the high steel frame over the open back of the truck for our lives for two and one half hours.

Orizaba is a beautiful mountain, but the stonewalled and tin-roofed Octavio Alverez hut is nothing to write home about. It's cold, filthy, and you share it with a very healthy population of mice. Their droppings cover the stone floor and wooden sleeping lofts. In the middle of the night one of the furry inhabitants woke me up when it paid me a nocturnal visit and crawled under and over my sleeping bag.

We began our ascent to the third highest summit in North America the next morning at 1:50. I was finally well acclimatized and felt great even with getting little rest the night before in the packed hut.

The route follows a steep trail with "no switchbacks" that leads past two aqueducts in disrepair and through a boulder field up to the Jamapa Glacier. On the glacier the slope levels off to approximately 30 degrees until one nears the volcano's crater, then the angle of ascent increases to about 40 degrees.

Unlike the confusing and exceeding long route on Izta, the climb is a straightforward slog to the top in good weather. Once we were on the glacier, I was sure the summit was in our grasp.

Then at approximately 17,000 feet or maybe higher, Dennis shouted up to Marko and I that Steve Broadie was in trouble again. Marko and I were tethered to a second rope a good hundred feet above the three of them.

The gentle slope of the glacier is deceiving, and any fall would quickly reach terminal velocity. I planted my axe in the hardened snow, clipped into it with a carabiner and sling already attached to my harness, and laid on top of it, while Marko descended to see what the problem was. When he reached them, he hammered in a picket and tied off to it for protection and then called for me to come down.

Apparently Broadie's rented double boots were too tight and his left foot had begun to freeze. When I arrived Marko was massaging Broadie's bare foot. Then he placed it on his stomach to help re-warm it. I figured our climbing was likely done for the day.

Frozen toes and whiteout conditions on Pico de Orizaba.
(Photo by author)

As it turned out we wouldn't have gotten much higher on the mountain anyway. A hideous storm suddenly materialized from around the other side of the volcano and as we huddled around our fallen comrade windswept sheets of water hit us. In a matter of seconds we were all encased in a thin layer of ice as the super chilled rain froze on impact. Then the visibility dropped to almost zero and the rain turned to a blinding snow.

Based on my previous, limited guiding experience Marko handed me his hammer, pickets, and ice screws and said, "Paul, lead the way down, and call out stop when you want to place a picket and yell go when you're ready to resume descending."

Leading a rope team over a glacier is daunting in any conditions. Making matters worst the ice-caked rope slowly grew to two inches in diameter and I began to wonder if it would hold if I fell into a crevasse.

The fog eventually became so thick I lost total sight of my companions. I knew they were somewhere behind me, but it seemed like I was wondering through the clouds alone. When the wind suddenly died it was dead silent except for the steady crunch, crunch of my crampons biting into the snow. The lack of wind helped Marko clearly hear me when I called out the signals he had instructed me to use.

Steve Broadie looked like a walking corpse and Steve Hunts was almost comatose when we finally made it down off of the glacier and back on the boulder field. Their faces were pasty white, their lips were turning blue, and they had that vacant stare. There was still 2,000 feet of slippery trail below us, and I thought for sure hypothermia was going to claim a victim or two.

Knowing Marko would have to continue to cajole the two of them to continue moving down the mountain, I quickly un-tied from the rope and took off at a run for the hut. Cristobal was still sleeping in the loft of the hut when I rushed through the door and started rummaging through gear to find Marko's stove. I eventually just started heating water for hot drinks on another party's stove that was already assembled and sitting on the hut's cooking surface.

Marko and my other three companions arrived about an hour later. We all downed cups of hot tea and then Marko made a big pot of hot soup. After consuming it, we took off our wet hats, our dripping outer shells, removed our muddy boots and climbed into our sleeping bags where we shivered until Joaquin, who wasn't scheduled to pick us up for four and one-half hours, arrived to take us back to Tlachichuca.

A pouring rain on the return drive down to Tlachichuca soaked us all again. I can still see Steve Broadie bouncing around, while laying in an inch or two of sloshing water, in the bed of Joaquin's big truck as we went over pothole after pothole.

A hot shower at Joaquin's revived us and the next morning Cristobal drove us to Teotihuacan -- the "City of the Gods". Miguel met us there and led us on a tour of the Platforms of the Sun and the Moon. The Toltecs (predecessors to the Aztecs) built the two platforms astride the Avenue of the Dead 2,300 years ago. Dennis and I ascended the hundreds of steps leading up to the top of the colossal Platform of the Sun. Standing on top of the Platform was an almost magical experience.

The highlight of this adventure was learning what the word hospitality really means from our Mexican hosts. We were welcomed into their homes and treated like visiting family members. I'll never forget them or my fun-loving teammates and Marko, who share my curiosity about the world and love of adventure.

ROCK AND ROAD TRIPS

After numerous vacations out West, including several trips to Estes Park, Colorado, I still had not experienced the excellent rock climbing on the elongated granite crag called Lumpy Ridge, which is located just above the popular resort town and within the boundary of Rocky Mountain National Park.

During the hot and dry August of 1994, I hooked back up with Marko Cornacchione and the two of us traded leads at Lumpy Ridge on the moderate climb called Batman Pinnacle. Marko then led a more difficult three-pitch climb appropriately called Bat Crack, where we could hear bats squealing in the big horizontal crack at the top of the first pitch.

The next morning Marko picked me up at my motel at 4:00. Our objective was to ascend the South Face of the Petit Grepon. The route is regarded as one of the fifty classic climbs in North America, and its one of the most popular rock climbs in Rocky Mountain National Park.

We beat two other rope teams to the start of the route that had chose to bivy overnight just below the climb. Marko led the entire climb and when he belayed me up onto the 11,400-foot high mountain spire's tiny tabletop summit it was 11:30 a.m.

We only spent minutes enjoying the view before we had to rappel off the tower and make a mad dash down the trail back to Marko's pickup to beat the usual afternoon thunderstorm. King-sized drops began to splat on his truck's windshield just as we left the Glacier Gorge Parking lot.

Later on during that same trip, my wife Judy and I drove to Jackson, Wyoming, where I soloed the South Teton car to car in nine hours. Afterwards, at almost 48 years old, I felt pretty cocky until I was told the record for ascending the Grand Teton car to car was something under three hours. When I got home I was anxious to return to Lumpy Ridge and did so in late June of 1995. It was a typical "rock and road" trip with four friends I'd met through the Iowa Mountaineer Club.

While camping in Rocky Mountain National Park we climbed at Lumpy three out of four days. On the last day I even put up a first ascent by accident. The five of us had been convinced that I was leading an easy route described in the guidebook. The name of the climb I thought I was on is Cottonmouth, and it has an easy rating of 5.5 on the rock climbing scale of difficulty that goes up to 5.14.

After struggling up a wet crack half-filled with dirt and moss that turned out to be to the right of the correct start to Cottonmouth I became a little desperate when I found myself on a rather vertical and absolutely blank section of rock. The dirty crack pinched out and my last nut placement was several feet below me.

Realizing the predicament I was in I looked down and froze. I was rather terrified of having to down-climb back to the ugly crack, and when I frantically searched the blank rock face above me for another placement my eyes locked on what looked like the actual belay stance for Cottonmouth, but it was well to my left and still 20 feet above me. I decided to go for it and held my breath until I reached it. Then I quickly slammed in a good cam and tied off to it.

Relived to still be in one piece, I shouted down to my companions, "5.5 my ass!" The name of the route stuck. And the next day a guide at the Colorado Mountain School assured me the variation I did wasn't listed in any guidebook and was likely a first ascent. I doubt if it's been repeated only because it's such an ugly route and includes what for me was a dangerous run out.

On the fourth day a cold and persistent rain drove us up to Vedauwoo near Laramie, Wyoming, where we were met by a thick fog and snow squall. After spending a night in a Cheyenne motel to dry out our tents we continued on up to the Black Hills, where we climbed for two days on the granite spires behind Mount Rushmore National Monument.

Climbs in the South Dakota Needles are notorious for having scary exposure and long run-outs. A lead climber who falls on such a route will likely make the next day's obituary page. Most of moderate routes, especially in the Mount Rushmore Area, now have bolts and good bolt anchors to provide for a safer climbing experience. But even on a well-bolted route a lead fall may result in stitches because the massive rock consists of exceptionally coarse pegmatite granite that is laced with jagged, sharp crystals of quartz and feldspar. The rocks friction is phenomenal, but it takes a couple of days for most visiting climbers to get used to using their fingertips and trusting their toes on the smaller crystals. It was actually my first experience with clipping a bolt and with what the climbing community calls "sport" climbing.

When I returned to work on July 5, I half-jokingly suggested to a young co-worker, David Panofsky, that we should drive out to the Black Hills some weekend. I could see that he took the bait but I didn't plan on having to pack anytime soon. David's wedding was scheduled for September.

On Thursday morning, July 20, David stood in the doorway of my cubicle with a catfish grin on his face and said, "I'll pick you up tonight at 7:00." I was convinced his fiancée, Pat Smith wouldn't approve and that he wasn't serious. I looked him in the eye and skeptically replied, "Yea right!" Half an hour later he had me asking my supervisor for that Friday off and calling my wife Judy to explain our plans. When I told her that David was picking me up after work to go to South Dakota there was a long pause on the other end of the line. I began to squirm like a worm on the end of a hook before she finally responded and calmly asked me, "Is their anything you'll need from the grocery store?"

I got home from work a little after 5:00, took a shower, gulped down a cheeseburger, and hurriedly packed. David and I were heading west on I-90/94 in his broken down Toyota by 7:30. There was so much rust around the headlights of his car that he had to brace them with sticks and use duct tape to keep them properly aimed. There was also a hole in the driver's side floor near the clutch. Somehow we safely arrived in Hill City with about two hours of rest on Friday morning at 7:00.

After eating the big breakfast at a local "hole in the wall" café we headed to the climbing area located behind Mount Rushmore and were pleasantly surprised to find ourselves alone on the pine-scented slopes dotted with the unique granite spires and outcrops. The only intrusion on our solitude was the helicopter, piloted no doubt by the mad Murdock character from the "A Team" and loaded with tourists, who likely had queasy stomachs and were a few dollars poorer. It and likely others buzzed the four presidential stone heads and us all day long.

I only knew the location of two climbs from my previous visit. But after consulting our newly purchased guidebook we jumped on a two-pitch climb called "Pipeline" that has a panoramic view from its summit. We also climbed the more difficult, 80-foot pitch on the same buttress called "Waves." It was one of the climbs I had led before.

Just when David was itching to attempt his first lead, the sky began to look threatening. I took him to the other climb I had lead previously called Sliding Sneakers or the Soloist; depending on which guidebook you happen to have. We hoped to stretch our luck but the weather just wouldn't cooperate. David climbed up to the third bolt on the route three times and had to delicately down climb each time because it began to rain. The weather kept teasing us and we probably gave up too easily, but we needed to head back to Hill City anyway for some provisions before finding a campsite. After buying ice and the makings for supper our departure from Krull's Supermarket was delayed by a torrential downpour that included marble-sized hail. In 15 minutes we could have scooped up all the ice we needed off of the parking lot for free.

The next morning David bagged his first on-site lead by climbing the route called Solitaire. The climb is quite easy until you get to a stance right below the last bolt. It's a very committing move to leave the stance and get above the bolt where a smooth, sloping handhold for your right hand exists and precious little for your left hand and your feet. Old and scary button bolts existed on the climb at the time, now it's been re-bolted with solid ¾ inch bolts, but the move above the last bolt is still as intimidating as before since a fall will result in a scary pendulum out over a 150-foot drop.

I couldn't see David from below but I could hear him mumbling. Then after a number of false starts he finally cast off and soon yelled he was off belay.

Then it was my turn to discover why he was so tenuous and what the delay was all about. As with most of the climbs in the Needles you have to have total confidence in the friction between the sticky rubber soles of your climbing shoes and the coarse face of the rock, but mentally coming up with the courage to make the final move on Solitaire is difficult. The reward for going for it is reaching its spectacular summit, which is 160 feet in the air and just big enough to mount like a horse.

We located and ascended three more routes that afternoon. One climb called Goatskin gave us both a scare. There are two almost overhanging sections on the climb between bolts where there are virtually no handholds and a couple of small crystals to place the tips of your toes on. While placing your entire weight on the very tips of your toes, you have to palm the rock with your hands to stay in balance. It's not very comforting to know that sometimes the protruding crystals break off. I had a huge one come right off in my hand earlier when I weighted it. I also learned why the climb was named Goatskin while belaying David up it when a Billy goat approached nearby.

That Saturday night on a lark we decided to break camp and drive to Devil's Tower National Monument in northeast Wyoming. We arrived at the Tower's campground at 7:30 p.m. and made plans to be up in the visitor center's parking lot by 5:30 on Sunday morning.

Devil's Tower consists of phonolite porphyry and probably isn't the eroded plug of a volcano like many people think, but an intrusion of magma that slowly cooled below the surface that was subsequently revealed by 60 million years of erosion.

In the early morning light the visually jarring monolith, which now stands over 1200 feet above the campground looks forbidding. Our palms began to sweat as we left the paved tourist trail and scrambled up to the base of the famous Durrance route, which is the easiest route to the top. I remembered experiencing the same nervous reaction six years ago when former climbing partner, John Preussner and I first stood at the base of the same climb.

I met John, who is an Iowa farmer in 1988 in a pub in Radium Hot Springs, British Columbia, while on my first Iowa Mountaineering Club trip. We hit it off immediately when he walked through the door, introduced himself, and then bought me a beer. After the trip ended we became climbing partners for a couple of years until he got hitched to his wife, Julie (the first couple to do so on top of Devil's Tower) and the two of them settled down to raising a family.

In 1989 the Durrance was the first unguided, multiple-pitch climb for both of us. Our ascent of the Tower turned out to be an eventful and memorable climb that we repeated four more times by different and more difficult routes with other climbers over the following week, while helping to lead a group of less experienced Iowa Mountaineer Club Members.

I was snapped back to the present task when David suddenly announced that a group of four other climbers were approaching. Andy Petefish, an old friend and owner of Tower Guides, appeared with three clients in tow. Andy and I greeted each other and then I asked David if he had me on belay.

The first pitch of the climb is 80 feet long and ascends one of the huge columns, known as "The Leaning Column". The very noticeable column is broken and leans against an adjacent column, thus its name -- The National park Service has recently determined that the leaning portion of the column is unstable and has warned climbers since 2006 that it could possibly topple at any time.

David paid out the rope from below as I advanced up the column mostly by stemming with my feet and hands. For non-climbers, a climber protects herself every now and then as she proceeds by wedging a nut or placing a camming device into a vertical crack between the columns. Then she has to attach a looped nylon sling to each piece of the protection she has placed with a carabiner and also to the rope with another carabiner. If for some reason she comes off of the rock, her belayer can stop her fall by using a braking device attached to the rope at his end and to his harness. If the piece of protection is well placed and holds, she'll fall twice the distance she's above it and the stretch of the climbing rope -- unless her partner isn't paying attention. In other words the belayer virtually holds his partner's life in his hands.

On the flat top of the leaning column there is a secure anchor system consisting of three bombproof bolts. After reaching the top of the column, I clipped into the anchor bolts and then belayed David up to me.

As the second climber on the rope it was his job to clean the route by retrieving the passive protection I had left behind. I in turn kept him on tension by taking in rope as he proceeded. That way if he were to fall he would only travel a few inches or a couple of feet because of rope stretch.

After David reached the top of the column and had also clipped into the anchor system, I took him off belay, re-stacked the rope, and retrieved my gear from him. He then placed me back on belay before I clipped out of the anchor system to lead the next pitch. In this way two climbers can free climb a route without driving pitons into a crack in the rock, hanging on any fixed or passive protection (aid climbing) or drilling bolts.

Before starting the second pitch, I decided to let Andy and his party pass by. I didn't want to be rushed or have any distractions while leading the 70-foot Durrance Crack, which is the hardest pitch of the route.

Author leading the Leaning Column Pitch.
(Photo by David Panofsky)

David and I were in the shade and we both began to shiver while we waited as the wind began to pick up. Finally Andy's clients - two of them were virtual beginners - passed through the pitch with the help of Andy's unique hauling technique.

There are two parallel cracks up the Durrance pitch. To ascend it you can use a combination of jamming and stemming techniques. When I began to advance up the pitch the strenuous effort of jamming my left foot into the crack on the left and stemming off of the dihedral's face with my right foot while jamming or stemming with my hands quickly warmed me. In complete contrast, higher up the route when we were in the direct sunlight drops of sweat literally ran down our foreheads into our eyes.

Near the top of the pitch where the footholds become less and less secure, each time I stopped to place protection my arms began to cramp. At the same time my concentration was being broken every time a Devil's Tower mini jet (cliff swallow) swooped by or pigeons landed on or flew off of adjacent columns.

Suddenly my right foot skated off of the rock. After struggling to regain my footing and balance, my legs began to quiver like Jell-O (an affliction climbers fondly refer to as sewing-machine legs). I thought I was going to have to take a lead fall and hoped David would be ready for the jolt on his end of the rope. Just then a large swallowtail butterfly floated by my face. It's serene beauty and effortless flight distracted me just long enough for me to regain my composure, and I quickly made two moves before mantling up onto the next belay stance.

It was David's first long climb and I knew he was quite intimidated by it. When his turn came to follow up the Durrance Crack, I just caught sight of his white helmet approaching near the top of the pitch right where I had struggled and then it disappeared.

I quickly caught his fall and while the rope immediately became taut I heard him exclaim, "Holy shit!" It was his first flight and it naturally left him a little shaken. But when he soon joined me at the belay he was wearing a big smile.

The third pitch of the climb is named Cussing Crack. It's a very short, ugly chimney that can become quite difficult or at least extremely uncomfortable and frustrating if you try to avoid the exposure out on the face of the rock and let yourself get drawn into it. The key is to avoid entering the narrow chimney. I learned that lesson the hard way in 1989 and later that same year on another much longer and more difficult climb called the Snaz, which is located in Death Canyon in Grand Teton National Park, near Jackson, Wyoming.

The Snaz is a beautiful, approximately 1600-foot long route put up by Yvon Chouinard. I struggled up its crux pitch, a difficult off-width crack, by jamming my hands or arms and feet into the crack. I was concentrating so hard on moving quickly up the pitch that my helmet crashed into the underside of the huge protruding roof at the top of it. A Jackson Hole Mountain Guide was belaying me from 20 feet above the roof and when I tried to get out from under the overhanging shelf of rock I was pulled off of the route by the taut rope. Not once but three times I swung like a pendulum out into the void several feet away from the rock wall. I wondered while I was swinging in the wind over 800 feet off of the deck if the rope was going to be cut by the sharp lip of the rock above me. Finally on my fourth try I was able to get back out from under the roof and grab a solid hold on the rock face to the right of it where I should have went in the first place.

This time on the Cussing Crack pitch I stayed totally out of the chimney and found the face climbing pretty easy. I then decided to continue on past the belay anchors at the top of the pitch to reach the next belay stance on top of the fourth pitch, an easy 40-foot long jam crack. Combining the two pitches saved us some time.

The fifth pitch is a very easy 40-foot chimney but I decided to ascend a more interesting looking crack to the left of it. The crack turned out to be two degrees harder. I also found myself 10 feet above the stance for the last and sixth technical pitch, which is a more difficult 15-foot lead called the "Jump Traverse." A fixed piton protects the jump move, which is situated above a 250-foot drop. After clipping a sling to the piton many climbers grab it while making the extremely exposed move. I started out too high and had to do just that to pull myself back to the start. David then held me while I leaned out over the drop to study the move. I quickly realized I just needed to go lower and then made the move with ease. David soon followed me and reached back across the gap to unclip my sling from the piton. It's an easy reach but he smartly backed himself up first by draping a sling over a protruding rock horn and clipping it to his harness.

I know of two climbers that have died while attempting to climb Devil's Tower. Several years ago a 16-year-old boy tried to solo the Durrance and ended up falling on the difficult second pitch down onto the top of the leaning column. The other climber fell to his death the first day Devil's Tower was re-opened to climbing after a voluntary June 1995 closure to allow Native Americans some privacy while they performed sacred rituals (Devil's Tower is considered by a number of the Plains Tribes to be sacred). Andy Petefish told me the climber was very experienced and was leading two others. Apparently he fell when he accidentally stepped on his rope and lost his footing while trying to retrieve his sling from the fixed pin at the Jump Traverse. If he had only taken the time to back himself up with a piece of protection as David had he would likely still be alive.

After the Jump Traverse the rest of the climb involves walking over a large grassy ledge called the "Meadows" to where the summit can be gained by an easy, albeit very exposed 165-foot scramble up to the top.

We topped out about 11:00 a.m., paused to exchange high five's, down some water, eat a snack and sign the register. The tablet for climbers to sign is kept in a large metal pipe next to a weathered post that marks the highest spot. The post is all that remains of a sign that once read, "No climbing beyond this point!" The sign used to be displayed in the climber's registration building adjacent to the visitor center.

The summit plateau is very flat and about the size of two football fields. It looks like a severely weathered, blacktop parking lot full of large cracks filled with weeds. The 360-degree view of the surrounding landscape is awesome and it seems like you are standing on an island in the sky.

A cairn or stone man (three or more rocks piled on top of one another) mark where the first rappel station -- two beefy bolts to thread the rope through -- can be found just below the rim. There are four rappels that are 150 to 160 feet long from the summit to the base of the Tower, and I wanted to get down before the clear, sunny weather changed.

Rappelling is the most dangerous part of climbing because you depend entirely on the anchor and your equipment as you slide down the ropes. When nearing the end of a rappel you also have to be careful that you don't overshoot the next rappel stance or worst slide off the

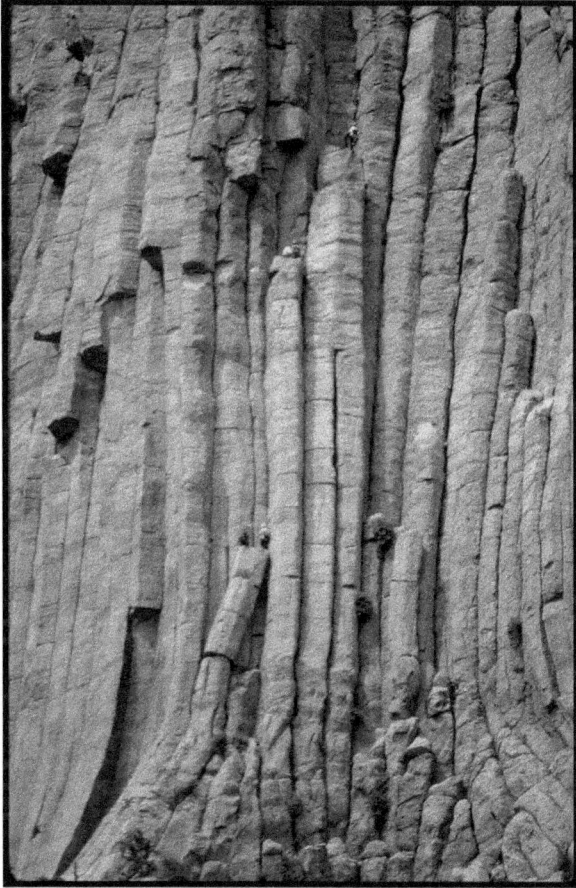

Climbers on the first three pitches of Durrance Route.
(Photo by author)

end of your ropes. Because of the length of the rappels climbers have to use two ropes to rappel. It's extremely important to remember which side of the rappel anchor the knot connecting the two ropes is on before pulling on one of the ropes to retrieve them for the next rappel. This is made easier by using ropes of different colors. That way you just have to remember the right color of rope to pull on. Otherwise, the knot connecting the ropes could get jammed in the rappel anchor. In such a predicament a climber has to either wait for an embarrassing rescue or risk climbing back up if he has a couple of prussik to free the knot (the former is a much safer alternative).

A good rappel or belay stance has at least enough room for a climbing party to stand on it. When there isn't a suitable stance at the end of a rappel or at the end of a pitch when ascending for that matter, a climber has to set up a "hanging rappel or belay anchor system." Fortunately, the rappel route down Devil's Tower has relatively roomy and flat stances that are at least two feet or more across at the end of each rappel.

It's a great relief to finally reach the base of the Tower and as soon as you do for some reason it's hard to believe that you actually stood on its summit. Once you are back on the paved path below the boulder field of fallen columns tourists immediately flock around you to ask if you went all the way to the top and what's up there. No, there is not a landing field for UFOs on top of the Tower or on its backside.

We quickly escaped the gaggle of tourists and enjoyed a couple of cold ones with Andy. David dropped me off at home in Portage, Wisconsin, on Monday afternoon at 3:15. On Tuesday morning I had to get up at 4:45 to go back to work in Madison.

The trip taught us what can be accomplished in three and one-half days. All you need is the ambition and desire to do what is considered out of the ordinary and by some maybe even crazy.

In fact, I've made the long one-day drive to Devil's Tower several times over the years, with friends I've climbed in the Black Hills Needles often enough that we're practically becoming locals – we've actually helped folks from Rapid City find routes.

Four of us (Lenore Sobota, the daughter and father duo of Anne and Dave Meyer, and myself) even nicknamed ourselves the "Rushmore Gang," while on one particularly memorable trip when we were determined to top out on Spire Four, which is located in the Cathedral Spires. The awe-inspiring formation is located about 1/2-mile from a small parking area on a hairpin corner of the famous Needles Highway (Hwy. 85). The most prominent spires are numbered, Spire one through Spire Nine. Spire Four is the high point of the formation.

We've had trouble not only locating the start to the standard route on Spire Four in past years, but when we finally did find it we were chased off of the route by bad storms.

Left to right the higher Cathedral Spires 2, 3 and 4.
(Photo by author)

The un-bolted route up the spire goes up a very wide but hidden chimney. At its top you must squeeze through a small opening (aptly named the "wormhole"), unless you choose an optional way around it to the left. While leading the climb I got stuck in the hole for about a half hour. Finally I worked my arms and shoulders back down out of the hole and escaped through the small gap un-roped only after taking off my glasses, helmet, chalk bag, all of my protection, my water bottle, rain jacket, and my harness. And when I emerged through the hole my pants were almost down to my knees. Lenore then came through it a few minutes later, and she exclaimed, "It was sort of like being born again, but nobody slapped me on the butt."

The third and last pitch of the climb is much more fun. But you have to make a "Leap of Faith" over a 700-foot drop from the top of the buttress you're on over to the main summit and the anchors/rappel station. It's what you call a very airy move.

The summit is at approx. 7,000 feet. It provides a 360-degree view of the Needles, the distant eastern Plains and the Badlands. Lenore was exhausted when we returned to the car, and it was a two-beer night for me when we got back to our campsite.

On the same trip, we did five new routes. Our favorite, besides the Spire 4 ascent, was a climb called Evarete. Like the approach to Spire Four, it took us a couple of years and several trips to find it. Ironically, it's just off of the main climbers approach trail to the biggest climbing area at Sylvan Lake. It has five bolts spaced about 20 feet apart and the first bolt is about 30 feet up, which used to be typical for the area.

Anne Meyer belaying author as he clips the first bolt on Evarete.
(Photo by Lenore Sobota)

It's an awesome climb that goes directly up a steep arête to a summit about one-foot wide. It also has a nice anchor at the top that provides a comfortable hanging belay, and the rappel back to the ground is partially free -- you can't touch your feet on the rock for about 50 feet. The rappel just adds to the fun of doing the route. We liked it so much we did it three times on the trip.

I also tired to do my first really difficult climb in the Needles, a climb called Tranquil Evening, rated 5.10. I came off just above the third bolt. It was my first fall in the Needles. The route is slightly overhanging at that point so no harm was done (no stitches were needed) except to my ego.

The long boring drive, sleep deprivation, bruises, sore back and shoulders, painful feet and peeling fingertips all quickly faded after we returned home.

WINTER PRACTICE

D evil's Lake State Park, nestled in the Baraboo Hills just south of the City of Baraboo, Wisconsin, is a Mecca for all of us unfortunate climbers residing in the relatively flat and rock exposure poor Upper Midwest. On any given weekend from early spring to late fall, just like the local wasps, we can be found swarming over the hard quartzite cliffs that tower above the unique lake formed by the last advance of the Green Bay lobe of the Wisconsin Glacier, when it left behind end moraines that blocked off the flow of an ancient river passing through the surrounding bluffs.

In sharp contrast, complete solitude can be enjoyed while climbing there in the winter. The first time I decided to try winter climbing at the park the morning's temperature was a brisk 25 degrees Fahrenheit and the night before a fast moving storm had left behind a coating of ice on top of a foot of snow. But it was also a bright, cloudless day and dead calm. The chilly air was so crystal clear that the rock buttresses on the East Bluff appeared to be 100 feet higher and the sunshine made every ice coated tree, bush and rock glisten as if they had been metamorphosed overnight into diamonds.

When David Panofsky and I stepped out of our cars in the south shore parking lot the silence was deafening. Even the normally raucous crows and numerous squirrels were nowhere in sight. The two of us shattered the eerie silence while approaching the Grottos Trail. The trail is named after the large depressions left behind along the toe of the large East Bluff talus field by an ice marginal stream as the Wisconsin Lobe Glacier receded from the area over 12,000 years ago. Plate-sized shards of the ice-covered snow broke beneath our boots with each step and pressure cracks also noisily zigzagged out in several directions. We had to stop moving to communicate.

We used ski poles for balance while ascending the iced over rock steps of the Potholes Trail, which is the steepest man-made access in the park to the top of the East Bluff. The trail, like many other trails and buildings in the park, was constructed in the 1930s by the Civilian Conservation Corps and takes its name from circular holes eroded in the quartzite near the top of the bluff by rocks swirling beneath an ancient waterfall.

We carefully traversed across the icy glaze covering the upper slope of the East Bluff back to the west towards the frozen lake just below where the trail winds through a cleft in the exposed Quartzite Formation called the "Red Rocks."

I remember joking with David, at the time that, "If one of us slips, it'll be a quick slide down to the big boulders in the talus field below us."

Our destination was the lowest point of the Doorway Rocks Formation, which is the start for a very easy and delightful two-pitch climb named "B-Minor Mass." Carrying full packs and wearing four layers of clothing and our double boots; free climbing any route that day was going to be a bit more dicey than normal. We considered it a good practice day for the real mountains.

When we reached the base of the climb, David decided to lead the first pitch. He stopped to coax the flow of blood back into his numbed fingertips after ascending the first 15 feet up to a comfortable stance. It was only his third lead climb and I suspected that his enthusiasm was beginning to fade almost as fast as the warmth radiated from his fingertips after their contact with the frigid cold stone.

Before making his next move he struggled to place his first piece of protection; a small camming device called a Friend in a vertical crack just above his head. Satisfied that the piece would stay put he positioned the toe of his right boot into a small icy indentation on the rock face, tentatively shifted his weight onto it and stretched to reach the first good ledge. Like everything else the flat ledge wore a thin veneer of ice and when he failed to find something, anything, to grab a hold of with his right hand, his right leg begin to shake uncontrollably. The Friend was well placed, but David and I both knew it wasn't going to keep him from landing in my lap if he came off. Suddenly his boot slipped off the small hold and somehow he managed to hang on to the rock face with his left hand. After two more half-hearted attempts to gain the ledge he sheepishly backed off and left it for me.

Having made the climb numerous times before in good weather and bad, whether obvious or hidden, each and every hold is familiar as an old friend. But I was also a little humbled when I was barely able to grasp the tenuous finger hold David didn't know about and haul my carcass up onto the ledge.

Ten vertical feet higher the route traverses to the left and then leads up a short, slightly overhanging face. Normally you just have to grab a good handhold that exists for the left hand and friction with your feet to stand up and reach the next ledge with your right hand. Trying to friction on the glass-like quartzite with double boots, however, was futile.

I instead scanned the blank face for any tiny edge to place a stiff boot on that I may have overlooked before. The rock face is pretty featureless and I finally had to lower myself back to a rest spot to shake out my tired left arm and to re-warm my fingers.

I was still feeling the effects of having injured my left arm four months earlier, while leading a nearby and moderately difficult crack climb called "Dippy Diagonal." I had felt the muscle fibers in the upper part of my arm part like the teeth in a zipper when the injury happened and I mulled over the consequences of tearing the muscle again.

Knowing we were all alone in the park, I was worried more than usual about falling. A large white pine is located right behind the sloping ledge and the vertical rock face below. A lead climber who pitched off from above the ledge would not only hit the ledge, but she would likely end up wedged between the rock buttress and the tree that hugs it. Imagining being stuck in such an embarrassing predicament brought a devilish smile to my face.

I finally just decided to go for it and was able to muscle myself up onto the next ledge. Lying there in the snow trying to catch my breath I felt and probably looked like a beached whale. I eventually constructed a solid belay and David soon joined me.

The second pitch of the climb consists of an inside corner with some great hand jams. The pitch is short but exposed and ends on top of a small platform called the "South Tower." On that unusual day the crack in the corner was partially filled with ice. I was finally able to slot one large wedged-shaped nut in a bombproof placement well above the belay anchors before committing to the jam moves leading to the top of the pitch.

When David joined me on top of the South Tower we both saw that the next pitch, which is actually another climb named "Flotsam and Jetsam" was totally draped in a curtain of ice. We wisely decided to call it a day, rappelled down an adjacent gully and carefully traversed back over to the Potholes Trail. On the noisy hike back to the parking lot we continued to marvel at the solitude and enhanced natural beauty the time of year and freak ice storm had provided us.

PAUL HUEBNER

RETURN TO VOLCAN CITALTEPETL

I n January 1996, I was asked to join a small group who planned to attempt Mt. McKinley (Denali) in Alaska in mid May. The cost of the trip would've been approximately $4500. Being chained like a dog for three weeks up on the crevasse-riddled Kahiltna Glacier and West Buttress Route with the likelihood of having to endure some of the worst weather on the planet weighed heavily on my mind.

Then at work one day David Panofsky and I discussed going to Argentina to climb Cerro Aconcagua instead. Aconcaqua is very near the Chilean border and is the highest mountain in South America and the Western Hemisphere at 22,834 feet. The normal route to its summit is non-technical and we figured we wouldn't have to incur the cost of joining a guided group. David, however, had no previous experience at high altitude. We therefore wisely set our sights a little lower and decided to go to Mexico to ascend El Pico de Orizaba, which is the 3rd highest mountain in North America. Only Denali and Mt. Logan in Canada are higher and at 18,850 feet, Orizaba (also known by its Aztec name Citaltepetl) would provide David a perfect entry-level experience to high altitude mountaineering. It would also give me the chance to reach a summit that had eluded me on my previous expedition to Mexico in 1994.

About 50% of the climbers attempting Orizaba make it to the top. If everything went well David and I reasoned we could always try Aconcagua the following year when he would be 30 and I'd be 50.

We were pleasantly surprised to find round trip airline tickets to Mexico City from Madison for $300. I estimated the rest of our expenses would be less than $200.

David speaks Spanish reasonably well so he made arrangements by phone to stay at the Hotel Gillow in Mexico City and to stay at a climbers dormitory owned by Señor Reyes in Tlachichuca, a small village near Orizaba. Señor Reyes has been hosting Orizaba climbers for over 50 years. He also provides transportation up to Piedra Grande where two huts are located on the north slope of Orizaba at 14,000 feet.

We planned to spend one night in Mexico City (el. 7,200 ft.), one night in Tlachichuca (el. 8,500 ft.), and two days and nights in one of the huts at Piedra Grande. On the fifth day we would bivouac at approximately 16,000 feet before making a bid for the summit. It was a sound plan if we both acclimatized well and the weather cooperated.

We arrived in Mexico City on Saturday, February 3, at 3:15 in the afternoon. After getting the green light through customs we each changed $150 into Pesos (The exchange rate was 7.4 Pesos to the Dollar). We then grabbed a taxi to the Hotel Gillow and were given a room that has two beds, a large tiled bath/shower, and a TV that broadcasts HBO and CNN in English. It only cost us a mere 190 Pesos ($26) a night.

The first task we had to perform was to find fuel for our camp stove. We had been told we could find gasolina blanca (white gas) at a paint store or hardware store. After spending about an hour searching up one block and down another we eventually stumbled across a hardware store only to have the owner inform us that he didn't have any gas for sale. He did, however, graciously give us directions to another store six blocks away that did. We located the store, made our purchase and returned to our room to fill our stove and spare fuel bottles. With that smelly chore completed we needed to find the City's East Side bus station and check schedules to the city of Puebla and to see if we could maybe even catch a direct bus to Tlachichuca.

We located the bus station on a map and found we could ride the subway (Metro Line 1) to San Larzaro, which would put us within two blocks of our destination. It cost a Peso to ride the modern Metro. At the enormous, circular bus station (called the "TAPO") we were quite astonished to learn that busses from a number of companies leave for Puebla every 15 minutes. Satisfied we could get an early start in the morning and hopefully reach Tlachichuca on another bus from Puebla before nightfall we returned to the Hotel Gillow -- riding the bus at night is not safe.

When we arrived back at the hotel David's aunt and uncle (Ruth and Alan Barnett) were waiting for us in the lobby. The two of them were returning from a human rights fact-finding trip in El Salvador and were in Mexico City enjoying the popular art, particularly the murals. On the slim chance that we could get together David had told them earlier of our plans. It was quite a coincidence to meet up with them because they were scheduled to fly back to the States in the morning.

The Barnett's insisted on taking us out to dinner. They took us to Sanborn's a famous restaurant that was the Zapotec Palace. Traditional blue, artistic ceramic tiles cover the outside of the three-story ornate building. The main dining room inside the former Palace is an open courtyard that features large crystal chandeliers, a beautiful fountain, and murals painted on the walls. The food was great. David and I planned to return.

Sunday morning we took a taxi back to the TAPO and purchased first class tickets for 29 Pesos ($3.90) to ride on a Pullman Plus of the Estrella Rosa Company. The windows of the plush coach were covered with dark purple curtains because the direct 90-minute ride includes an American movie in English and subtitled in Spanish.

At the Puebla bus station we were relieved to learn that a bus leaves for Tlachichuca every 30 minutes. We looked at each other and laughed, the second-class bus we eventually rode fit all of the normal conceptions of a bus in the third world. Virtually every window in the faded red coach was damaged and a spider web of cracks surrounded a bullet hole in the windowpane next to my head. The seats were dirty and worn, the back of David's seat was sprung, and the busses transmission sounded like it was going to drop onto the roadway every time the driver shifted. The brakes whined and the interior of the bus filled with the pungent smell of hot asbestos each time the driver hit the brake petal. The only thing missing was the stereotypical old woman carrying a live pig or chicken aboard.

On the way to Tlachichuca we stopped anywhere locals happened to be standing along the highway or whenever a passenger signaled the driver with a whistle, which either meant someone wanted to get off or someone was running across a field to get on. At every designated stop as soon as the bus ceased moving and the driver opened the door children jumped on and rushed through the aisle peddling sandwiches, candy, or sodas. They barely had time to canvas the packed bus before it resumed moving. It took us four hours to travel about 100 miles.

In stark contrast to the stadium-sized facilities in Mexico City and Pueblo, the bus station in Tlachichuca is a small bare room. There were a dozen plastic chairs placed along two of the plain, dirty white walls and a little table sitting in one corner covered with a stack of yellowing papers along with hand copied schedules. But when we stepped through an open doorway it was like suddenly entering another world. The streets of Tlachichuca were bustling with activity and the Village Square was filled with the colorful Sunday market.

Not knowing where the store associated with the Reyes family was located we stood on the sidewalk with a lost look on our faces until a taxi appeared and the driver politely told us the store was just two blocks down the street. We went back inside the bus station to quickly unpack our duffel bags, load our backpacks for more mobility, and then walked to the Reyes store. Heads turned as we passed and everyone watched with curiosity as the two of us waddled down the street burdened by our huge loads.

When we reached the store I stayed outside to watch our belongings, while David went inside to inquire about our reservations. He was greeted by a five-year-old girl who proceeded to lead him to a circuitous corridor that leads to the courtyard inside the Reyes compound. As he entered the courtyard, Herrardo Reyes Rodriquez Carlin emerged from his house. Herrardo is a general surgeon with a practice in Mexico City. We just called him Doctor. Later we also met his beautiful wife Carina and their two little daughters, Anna Carolina and Maria Theresa.

The main building of the Reyes compound is a large two-story structure that used to be a soap factory. Some of the unique and, I might add, antique machinery for making bars of soap still remains inside. The lower level contains several long tables for climbers to sort their equipment, a large covered table to prepare food, a sink and a gas stove for cooking, and a pot-bellied stove surrounded by comfortable chairs and a sofa to encourage socializing with other climbers. Upstairs where shoes and food are not allowed, there are about a dozen large comfortable bunk beds fitted with sheets and heavy wool blankets. A modern shower house and two bathrooms are located in an adjacent building. The fee is $10 a night and included coffee and homemade breads and cookies delivered by Carina each morning.

The next day after exercising a burro, a couple of horses, and working on a jeep wagoneer our driver Ariel drove us up to Piedra Grande in an old army truck. The trip to Piedra Grande is a ride to remember. You have to travel on a narrow, dirt track that steeply rises 5,500 feet in 14 miles. The last time I made the trip in 1994 it had just rained. This time it was bone dry and the four-wheel drive truck kicked up so much dust we covered our faces with a bandanna. At the end of the ride our packs and the two of us were coated with a layer of volcanic dust.

At Piedra Grande we met two young Mexican climbers from Monterrey who were staying in the big Octavio Alvarez hut. Two other groups were just leaving for Tlachichuca. One group of four Americans rode back down with Ariel. The other group, which consisted of six climbers from Mexico City, left in their own truck.

We decided to occupy the older and smaller Augusto Pellet hut located just upslope. We were fortunate to have the corrugated metal building all to ourselves. It has held as many as 12 climbers but I'd have been claustrophobic if there had been four.

After settling in we filled our water containers at a nearby spring. The Doctor had told us the water is okay but we filtered it anyway just to be on the safe side. We forced ourselves to drink three to four liters of water a day not including hot drinks and meals. Staying well hydrated at high altitude keeps the body healthy, but it also leads to the unpleasant chore of having to get up in the middle of cold nights. As usual due to the altitude I was only getting a few hours of actual shuteye each night since leaving home. Despite having a head cold David seemed to sleep fairly well.

We took an exploratory hike Tuesday morning after a leisure breakfast to help us acclimatize to the altitude and to search for a potential bivouac site. We hiked up the lower part of the well-worn trail leading to the Glacier de Jamapa. The trail steeply goes up a prominent gully towards two stone aqueducts. When we reached the second aqueduct we left the main trail and traversed towards the east to a ridge I knew from my last visit had some potential flat and dry sites.

We scrambled up the ridge and eventually found a number of fairly flat sites near 15,500 feet that offered some protection from the wind. We then descended to spend another night at the hut.

That afternoon David's cold worsened. Fortunately, a group of Americans led by a Mexican Guide working for the American Alpine Institute had arrived and David was able to bum a sleeping pill off of one of them. After taking it he slept soundly the entire night. I had another fitful night and became concerned that the insomnia was draining my strength.

On Wednesday morning we left the hut just before 11 a.m. and headed for the potential bivouac sites we scouted out the day before. At the second aqueduct we changed our minds and decided to continue up the trail to find a higher camp.

Just above the second aqueduct the trail takes a sharp turn to the west and climbs up past a series of dark cliffs to a rocky moraine that leads to a small, bare valley. At the end of the valley the only true flat area is on top of a small moraine right below a steep snow covered headwall that leads to the toe of the glacier. A tent belonging to two men from Liechtenstein already occupied it.

Not having a tent we dropped our packs and rushed to build stonewalls around a large boulder to provide some shelter from the wind as the sun dipped below the valley wall. Our chosen bed for the night was not level.

After chopping enough ice to melt for water, inhaling a bowl of soup, and draining the last drops of tea from our insulated mugs we crawled in our sleeping bags and bivy sacks. We set our wrist alarms for 3:30 a.m. The sky was clear and a full moon all week promised to light our way until sunrise.

I closed my eyes but sleep was out of the question. The wind quickly died down and it wasn't terribly cold, but it was an all night struggle to keep from rolling down slope. Some time well after midnight a mouse ran across my face. It was headed Dave's way and to my relief and satisfaction proceeded to bother him. About 2 a.m., we both agreed it was the most uncomfortable night either of us had ever spent. We should've just got up and headed up the mountain.

When our alarms went off, David dutifully arose and chopped some more ice for water. When he handed me my mug filled with hot chocolate I was still in my bag. I didn't feel a bit guilty. I just cradled the warm plastic container in my hands and told myself age is supposed to have some privileges. It was 5:30 a.m. before we finished another round of hot drinks, filled our water bottles, stashed our extra equipment and had our crampons on.

We roped up when we reached the top of the headwall. From that point on the climb is a 3,000-foot slog up the snow covered Jamapa Glacier.

We climbed to where the glacier's slope increased to about 35 degrees. I looked back at Dave and it was a long way down to the bottom. The snow was very hard but there wasn't any ice. I saw some partially open crevasses, and a couple of times the hollow bright-blue hole that remained when I pulled my axe out of the snow revealed other hidden ones. I placed a number of aluminum pickets to help safeguard us.

Climbing Orizaba, like any big mountain, is a challenge that is as much mental and psychological as it is physical. I wasn't very optimistic about our chances of reaching the summit because I hadn't slept more than 18 hours in the last 100. It wasn't very long before our legs became heavy, our hearts were galloping, and our chests were heaving. We continued to struggle upward, one breath, one step at a time.

I was more relieved than anything when the interior of the relatively compact crater fell away for several hundred feet beneath our feet. It was 12:30 p.m. and we were one and half-hour behind our schedule. I also knew our suffering had only begun.

The view was as we expected. You could see well beyond Puebla to the west and we could have seen the Gulf of Mexico to the east if low-lying clouds hadn't concealed it.

Concerned that we would miss our scheduled 4 p.m. pickup back at Piedra Grande, we dropped off of the summit and began the long tiring descent. The snow was still frozen and we had to check our momentum with each step downward.

When we returned to our bivouac site to retrieve the equipment we had left behind, David packed up quickly and left to try to get down before Ariel decided to leave us. After a short rest I hoisted my pack on and got back on the trail, but my legs eventually became loose and almost uncontrollable. In the valley I just bounced from one brief landing to another and the only thing pushing me downward was the weight of the pack on my back. About halfway down the rocky trail within the valley two of the footfalls I searched out ahead and committed too rolled under my weight. I did a complete somersault and found myself laying on the trail laughing at myself and trying to decide if I should just stay there and become vulture bait or get up and continue punishing my burning quads.

When I reached the second aqueduct I saw the army vehicle far below parked next to the main hut. David and Ariel were standing next to it watching my slow progress. Unfortunately, I slipped again and wrenched my right knee. After that I had to support every painful step with my ice axe. I tried to ignore the pain and occupy my mind by thinking about the restaurant meal I would have and the comfortable bed I'd be sleeping in that night.

On the way down to Tlachichuca we passed a group of Mexicans, mostly teenagers, milling around three large parked trucks. We later learned that the teens were from a nearby city and were on a prep school field trip. When we initially drove by I noticed a girl lying on the ground. She looked to be in pain and was being tended by three very concerned looking adults. I looked at Ariel and said, "Altitude?" He responded, "Si, altitude!" He then shook his head back and forth as if to say, "People just don't seem to understand that you can't just run up the mountain." At that point on the road the elevation was about 12,000 feet.

About a mile further down the road a large dust cloud approached us. When we were nearly side-by-side a man driving a pickup truck waved for us to stop. After a short conversation with Ariel the pickup proceeded up the road. Ariel then turned to David and asked him if the two of us minded going back to get the girl we had seen. Apparently she was seriously ill. Of course we both said, "No problem."

When we returned we were surprised to find a number of the kids sick. About a dozen were eventually loaded into the open back of the military truck. Two were unconscious, several of the others were passing in and out of lucidity, and the girl we had seen previously was totally delirious. Not knowing what was happening to her or even where she was, she screamed and cried every time she awoke. When a boy vomited blood, I realized they weren't just suffering from acute mountain sickness, but probably had cerebral edema and unless they got down to a lower altitude quickly they would die.

David and I felt completely helpless. There was nothing to do but hang on as Ariel, realizing the seriousness of the situation, drove as fast as he dared. He deftly dodged trees, rocks and huge holes that made the drive a difficult challenge even in daylight.

Gravel and dust flew as we rounded a sharp corner near the turnoff to the village of Hildago, which is probably the highest community in North America at 11,155 feet above sea level. Minutes passed like hours as we raced down the winding excuse for a road and slowly lost elevation.

Ariel speeded up when we reached the outskirts of Tlachichuca. We roared down a couple of side streets, narrowly missed colliding with a parked car as we rounded a sharp corner, and then suddenly slid to a stop in front of what looked like a relatively new, one-story building. Above a large glass door a single bare bulb illuminates the words, "Cinica Rural" or country clinic. Ariel jumped out, ran to the door and pounded on it. A lone nurse tentatively opened the door and the kids who couldn't walk were carried inside.

When Ariel delivered us to the Reyes compound it was quite late. We washed up and decided to see if the Casa Blanca, a recommended restaurant, was still open. When we knocked on the locked door of the restaurant we interrupted an old woman that was watching a soap opera on a tiny black and white television. She let us in and for 44 Pesos told us to help ourselves to a beer and served us a plate of scrambled eggs and fried potatoes with black beans and tortillas on the side.

Before dozing off that night and finally getting a good night's sleep my mind replayed the wild ride down from Piedra Grande. It had been an unexpected and involuntary race between life and death that ended in a photo finish. I'm still not sure I want to know if anyone lost.

We returned to Puebla in the morning and arrived back in Mexico City in the early afternoon. We celebrated our successful climb that Friday night at Sanborn's by having our most expensive meal of the trip (several large mouth-watering shrimp, french fries, two beers and coffee, which cost us about $7 a piece).

Saturday morning we took a bus to the Zona Arqueologica de Teotihuacan. The round trip to the 2,000-year-old "City of the Gods" only cost 16 Pesos or about $2.13.

We returned to Mexico City about 2 p.m., and went shopping for crafts. After a fine meal at the Restaurante Vegetariano we polished off the evening conversing with a young Canadian from Calgary, while sipping $0.50 bottles of Negra Modelo's at a table under an umbrella outside a Shaky's Pizza across from the Zocalo and Metropolitan Cathedral.

Sunday morning we had a fine breakfast at the Cafe Popular, and before catching our 3:15 p.m. flight to Chicago we took the Metro to Chapultepec Park. We wanted to visit the renowned National Museum of Anthropology, but there was a long line waiting to get in when we arrived. Admission to all of the museums in Mexico City is free on Sundays. Not having the time to wait in line we wandered over to a nearby field and spotted six, brightly dressed Aztec performers. One of them took up a collection from the crowd that gathered. Then as we craned our necks they proceeded to scale a 100-foot steel pole. One man climbed up onto the very top where he sat on a small seat and played a flute. The other five stood on a steel ring attached to the pole just below its top and coiled thick ropes around the top section of the pole, which rotates. When they finished wrapping the ropes around the pole and had secured themselves to the loose ends of the ropes with a bowline knot, they jumped off of the steel ring they were standing on. As the top section of the pole rotated, the ropes slowly unwound as the five men spiraled around the pole all the way down to the ground.

On the flight home I thought about how David and I are different in profound ways. He's a vegetarian. I'm not. He speaks fluent French and Italian and enough Spanish to get by. I know about ten words in Spanish. He's a classical musician and plays a mean violin; I can't even carry a tune. At the time David was 29 and I was 49. And finally, he's a diabetic. The one thing we share in common is we both love to climb. As expected we had some minor disagreements, primarily over food. In one short week, however, this was one of the best adventures either of us ever had.

GAMBLING ON COTOPAXI

After climbing Orizaba the previous winter, David Panofsky and I again put off Aconcagua and considered returning to Mexico to ascend Iztaccihuatl (17,343 feet). While firming up our plans we discovered American Airlines was offering round trip tickets from Chicago to Quito, Ecuador for $564. We quickly changed our plans and decided to go to Ecuador to attempt Cotopaxi, which at 19,348 feet is the loftiest active volcano in the world.

The week before our scheduled flight, Ecuador ousted its flamboyant president, Abdala Bucaram (aka El Loco), and a three-way fight for the presidency threw the small Andean country into political turmoil. We almost canceled our trip after watching CNN broadcasts of violent demonstrations taking place on the streets of Quito and reading newspaper headlines announcing that American Airlines' pilots were threatening to go on strike the morning after our flight was to arrive in Quito.

Then just two days before we were to leave the troubles in Ecuador were temporarily resolved. Bucaram had fled to Panama and the Ecuadorian Congress voted its leader Fabian Alarcon, interim president until elections could be held in August of 1998.

We left O'Hare as scheduled on Thursday, February 13, and later that evening we departed Miami's International Airport on the last American Airlines flight to leave for South America before the strike deadline. We landed at Quito's International Airport at 11:20 p.m.

Outside the Quito terminal we failed to follow one of our golden rules when traveling. Instead of looking for gray hair when picking a taxi driver we let a young assertive man from the crowd lead us to his cab. The minor slip could have cost us more than just a few extra Sucres (the Ecuadorian currency). The exuberant cabby ignored red lights while driving down the main drag -- Quito's showpiece street, Avenida Amazonas. He even used the sidewalk at one intersection to pass the law-abiding motorists who had stopped.

David quizzed the cabby in Spanish about his country's recent political troubles. "Bucaram is crazy and his government was very corrupt!" he exclaimed sarcastically. "He filled his cabinet with family members and business friends and funneled millions of dollars from our treasury out of the country. Then he promoted as an economic austerity measure raising the prices for fuel and utilities 300%." For emphasis, he waved one and sometimes both hands in the air. A couple of times he actually turned around to face us. I couldn't help but notice the speedometer was registering a constant 85 km/hr (a little over 50 mph). Fortunately, the streets near midnight were nearly deserted.

Graffiti on several buildings was the only visible reminder of the violent street protests we had viewed on CNN the week before. "Do you think we should be concerned about future work stoppages or protests?" David inquired. "No. You don't have to worry," the taxi driver assured us. "Everybody is happy Alarcon is now president. They will wait to see what he will do."

Nearing our destination the cabby abruptly changed lanes and slammed on the brakes to avoid a near collision. He then turned sharply onto the narrow side street named Foch where he finally had to slow down to search for the "Magic Bean," which was to be our home for the next three days. He soon spotted the large, colorful sign advertising the small two-story cafe/hostel, accelerated and sped across the intersection of Foch and JL Mera without looking for oncoming traffic and screeched to a halt at the curb. He then jumped out of his cab, extracted our bags out of his trunk, and ran up to the large wrought iron gate barring the entrance to a covered outside terrace. There he rang a bell to announce our late arrival.

A muscular black man in fatigues and carrying a crude sawed-off shotgun greeted us. We identified ourselves; paid the cabby an exorbitant fare, and the night guard unlocked the gate and gave us an armed escort inside.

A coworker had recommended the Magic Bean to us. It was currently the most popular international meeting place in "New Town" Quito. Our double room included a shower, lots of storage space and a continental breakfast for $24 a night. The coffee is great and they serve a frozen cappuccino pie to die for.

We had planned on sleeping late Friday morning, but made the mistake of going to bed without inserting earplugs. Once the early rush hour traffic began it sounded like the entire city of two million were driving to work right through our bedroom.

Our first priority after breakfast was to exchange some dollars. A short walk took us back to Avenida Amazonas where the modern hotels, banks, and many of the more fancy restaurants and shops are located. We both exchanged $100 at the first casas de cambio (exchange house) we encountered and received 367,500 Sucres apiece.

Not having a pocket calculator with us, it was impossible to figure out what something actually cost in dollars. Back in our room David calculated that: 50,000 Sucres approximately equaled $15.00; 20,000 Sucres was about equal to $6.00; 10,000 Sucres was almost $3.00; and so on. He then made handy little cheat sheets for us to carry in our pockets.

At an elevation of approximately 9,350 feet Quito is the second highest capital in South America after La Paz, Bolivia. The confined city fills a large highland valley approximately 40 miles south of the Equator.

That afternoon we decided to go to the Instituto Geografico Militar (IGM) to purchase some topographic maps. The IGM is situated on top of a large hill just above Parque El Ejido, a large tree-shaded park at the end of Avenida Amazonas. While ascending the steep hill the first thing we noticed besides the effect of the altitude was the intensity of the equatorial sun. The humidity wasn't bad and the temperature was a mild 74 degrees Fahrenheit, but the sun directly overhead made it feel almost tropical.

Like in Mexico the previous year our next errand turned into a scavenger hunt. We wanted to find and purchase fuel for our camp stove. We had borrowed a stove that burns butane from a coworker because both white gas and kerosene are impossible to find in Ecuador. The stove was a new model and after stopping in several outdoor stores we realized that the newer canisters needed to fit the stove had not arrived in Ecuador. A day later I relented and purchased an older model stove and two butane canisters.

Saturday morning we splurged on a breakfast buffet at the five-star Hotel Oro Verde. The buffet and view from the hotel's elegant restaurant were superb. The tab, however, equaled a night's lodging at the Magic Bean.

That afternoon we toured the Casa de la Cultura Ecuatoriana, which is Quito's best archaeology museum. It's a beautiful circular glass building that contains an awesome display of pottery, gold ornaments, and early religious to contemporary modern art. The display was quite fascinating and very educational. In particular, the size and complexity of the Inca Empire just prior to the Spanish Conquest amazed us. After completing the tour, we hopped on a local bus. For 400 Sucres (about 10 cents) we rode into "Old Town" Quito. We wanted to see some of the colonial architecture Old Town is renowned for.

We stepped off the local bus onto a side street in what can only be described as a bad neighborhood. Immediately we both felt vulnerable, which is unusual for someone as well traveled as David. We walked as fast as we could through a dark tunnel and up a long stairway that led to Guayaquil, a main thoroughfare.

From Guayaquil, we went up another side street and climbed several flights of steps to the top of a very steep hill to get a close up view of the new church, La Basilica. The spectacular church has been under construction since 1926.

From the church we walked several blocks to the Plaza de la Independencia. It felt a little weird standing in front of the Presidential Palace knowing that only the week before it had to be protected with extra troops and barricades of sandbags and barbed wire. We chose an old, gray-haired taxi driver to drive us back to the Magic Bean.

We wanted to do a conditioning hike in the Pasochoa Forest Reserve on Sunday. The small private reserve is managed by the Fundacion Natura and is located approximately 18 miles southeast of Quito near the village of Amaguana. It's a bird sanctuary and one of the last remaining stands of undisturbed highland cloud forest in Ecuador. The luxuriant forest is entirely within the northern flanks of Pasochoa's extinct caldera. The southern half of the caldera blew away in a violent eruption thousands of years ago.

There is a simple hostel, picnic areas, and several maintained trails in the reserve. One trail leads out of the lush forest onto the treeless Paramo (high pampas) almost to the summit of Cerro Pasochoa (13,780 feet). We intended to go to the summit - a six to eight hour round-trip hike from the reserve's headquarters.

We were going to take a bus to Amaguana. From the village we then hoped to catch a local taxi or hitch a ride up to the reserve's entrance. I was concerned we wouldn't have enough time to complete the summit hike and return to Quito before nightfall. Riding a bus to anywhere in Ecuador is amazingly cheap but traveling after dark in the countryside or in Old Town is asking for trouble.

I suggested to David that perhaps we should take a taxi to at least Amaguana, if not the whole way to the Pasochoa Forest Reserve. Another possible alternative would be to join a small group on a jeep tour. Our Lonely Planet guidebook titled, "Ecuador & the Galapagos Islands," recommended "Safari Tours," a company, which specializes in jeep transport to anywhere in Ecuador. After discussing our options we agreed to check with the Tour Company.

In a tiny branch office of Safari Tours, Jean Brown, who is a verifiable encyclopedia on traveling in Ecuador, greeted us. "Pasochoa is a bad choice for a conditioning hike," Brown said after we described our strategy to use Pasochoa as a warm-up hike and asked her if a group was scheduled to travel there by jeep on Sunday. "The trails in the reserve are rugged and very steep." She checked some schedules and informed us that all of the company's jeeps were booked full for Sunday.

We asked her for a recommendation. "Well, you could spend a couple of days at the Hacienda San Jose De El Chaupi," She replied with certainty. "It's really easy to get there. All you have to do is grab any bus heading south on the Pan-American, jump off at Machachi and catch a local bus from there to the town of El Chaupi. From the town's square it's an easy walk on a cobble stone road up to the hacienda. The hacienda is located at 11,000 feet, which is the perfect elevation for sleeping while acclimatizing. And, you can do day hikes on a dirt road that leads almost the entire way up to the refugio located in the saddle between Iliniza Sur (17,268 feet) and Iliniza Norte (16,818 feet)."

Brown handed me a photo album containing pictures of the hacienda's interior and of the Ilinizas. She then helped another customer while David and I browsed through the album. The hacienda looked like a pleasant place to spend some time and the pictures of the area around the Ilinizas refugio looked spectacular.

"The hacienda is a dairy farm owned by a wonderful man named Rodrigo Peralvo," Brown explained after helping a European woman plan a trip to the Galapagos Islands. "The cost for the night and a great breakfast is only $10."

We still wanted to hike up Pasochoa and our original itinerary called for spending the three nights at a hotel in the city of Latacunga, which is located along the Pan-American about 35 miles south of Quito and near Cotopaxi National Park. We instead decided to stay at the hacienda, Monday through Wednesday.

Brown called Rodrigo to let him know we would be arriving early Monday afternoon. She also made arrangements with him for us to get a ride early Thursday afternoon to Cotopaxi National Park.

Before hitting the sack that night David asked the night guard to have a taxi pick us up at 6 a.m. The taxi arrived right on time. When we told the middle-aged cabby we wanted to go to Amaguana, he demanded $100 to take us there. It was apparent from the expression on his face and the vagueness in his eyes that he didn't have a clue on how to get there. David explained that it was only an 18-mile drive. We then tried to bargain the fare down to $20, which was the maximum price the two of us agreed to spend for a taxi the night before. The crafty man studied us. "Fifty dollars!" he countered. We threatened to take a bus. "No! No! You don't want to take a bus," he quickly replied. "Thirty dollars! I drive you for $30." We reluctantly agreed.

On the way to Amaguana he dodged pigs, played chicken with every kind of vehicle imaginable, and traveled up to 140 km/h (about 84 mph) when going downhill. He also pulled over three times to ask for directions. Eventually we were dropped off above Amaguana on the one lane cobble stone road leading to the Pasochoa Forest Reserve. Before letting us go, the cabby shook us down for another $10. Adding further insult to injury we still had to walk three miles to get to the reserve's entrance. We surmised that he drove away one very happy man.

The reserve is beautiful and exotic. Little sunlight penetrates the dense canopy of the forest and muddy trails bore through the jungle-like vegetation like a tunnel. A couple of times we had to almost get down on our hands and knees to proceed.

The trail to the summit skirts the boundary of the reserve and in places is lined by tall thickets of bamboo. It goes straight up slope. There are no switchbacks.

It was very humid inside the forest. Each time we pushed away a clinging, moss-covered vine or oversized leaf a shower of water droplets mixed with our sweat. Half expecting to be devoured by bugs we were amazed that there were none. We saw colorful orchids and could hear many different kinds of birds calling. Trying to spot the birds while on the move and without binoculars was futile.

The dense vegetation increased our anticipation for the view we knew we'd have when we finally popped out onto the grassy Paramo.

The view was worth the effort and the wait. We could see the city of Machachi far to the south and Amaguana below us. The entire countryside was a collage of green fields and forest. It would've been even better if clouds hadn't concealed the huge snow-capped peaks to the south located along what Ecuadorians refer to with pride as "the Avenue of the Volcanoes."

Up on the Paramo the trail became indistinct. We just continued straight up through the knee-high grass.

We encountered a fairly wide trail (actually it was a firebreak) on top of the ridge formed by the rim of the ancient caldera. After taking a brief rest we followed the dirt path along the ridge and up a long grassy slope that ended at the base of a near vertical rock wall. When we reached that point the contours on our topographic map indicated that we were standing at an elevation of approximately 13,000 feet.

David wanted to get a closer look at the actual summit, which was in the clouds and still about 780 feet above us. It started to sprinkle and some ugly dark clouds were rapidly closing in on us from the north. I wasn't about to scramble up the exposed rock in the rain. We were miles from help and the wall was very near the rim. One slip while ascending or descending the wall could result in a nasty tumble. Quite possibly, one would even go over the nearby edge of the calderas. I waited behind while David disappeared over the top of the wall and it started to rain harder. David finally reappeared just as I was getting ready to leave for the protection of the forest canopy. It poured on us all the way back to where we first topped out on the ridge. Then it let up.

While descending the steep muddy trail through the reserve, I was experiencing quadriceps death. We arrived back at the reserve's headquarters at 2:30 p.m. After another brief rest we started walking the four miles back out to the highway.

It poured, then it stopped, and then it poured harder. Between the on again, off again showers, the sun played "peek-a-boo" with the clouds. Our clothes and the road steamed each time the sun revealed itself.

Our spirits were further dampened when all of the cars leaving the reserve drove by us. Most of them were full. We were wet and muddy and really didn't expect them to stop. We stuck out our thumbs anyway.

Finally with about a mile to go a local man allowed us to jump in the back of his pickup. David gave him a "Clif Bar" when he dropped us off at the highway.

We waited soaking wet on the shoulder of the highway for what seemed like more than the half-hour it was before a bus appeared. We were barely able to squeeze on the packed vehicle. The claustrophobic ride back to Quito only cost $1.50.

Back at the Magic Bean I ordered a large bottle of the local Pilsner and the "Tuna Kabob" dinner, which consisted of roasted green and red peppers, onions, and at least a pound of delicious fresh tuna on two skewers. I was also served lots of seasoned fried potatoes and garlic bread on the side. I ate until my stomach was like a balloon ready to burst. We both wanted to sample a dessert but had no room left after finishing our main course.

Before going to bed we packed for our trip to the hacienda. We left behind what we could but our backpacks still weighed over 70 pounds.

In the morning we took a taxi to the Terminal Terrestre (main bus station), which is located in Old Town. The driver dropped us off in the back of the station next to a bus getting ready to leave for Machachi. We were expecting to have to hoist our heavy packs up on top of the bus. Instead, the assistant motioned for us to jump aboard. The rest of the passengers were amused as we struggled to squeeze through the narrow folding door. I felt like one of the "three stooges" when either my large double plastic mountain boots, ski poles or sleeping pad strapped to the outside of my pack momentarily hung up on the door.

Traveling down the three lane Pan-American was another hair-raising experience. The bus driver preferred the middle lane. Fortunately, oncoming traffic yielded to the bus but not until the last minute, and only after the bus driver laid on the horn. David chose a seat near the back of the bus. I did the opposite and took a seat in the front row. I'd rather see what's coming, even if it's impending doom.

The bus dropped us off at an intersection just outside of Machachi where we could catch local buses leaving the city. The first El Chaupi bus to appear was crammed. Heads and arms were literally sticking out of its windows and the passenger doorways. We let it and the next one, which was also full pass by.

Before the next bus came along a small white pickup leaving the city turned onto the highway. The driver looked at me as he drove by. I returned his gaze and he must have read my mind. He pulled over and offered to drive us to El Chaupi for $5.00. He was an excellent driver. It was the safest six miles we traveled in Ecuador.

The little highland community consists of a dozen buildings constructed around a small dirt square. After figuring out which of the other three roads leading out of town to take, we hoisted our packs and starting walking. About a quarter of a mile out of town another white pickup stopped when it reached us. It was Rodrigo. After introductions we jumped in the back of his truck with our packs. He apologized three times that the front seat was fully occupied by his two beautiful, white Samoa dogs. They crowded him in the seat and go everywhere with him.

Rodrigo is one of the hardest working and nicest men I've ever known. His day starts at 4 a.m. The only time I ever saw him sit down was to eat a meal or to enjoy a good fire just before going to bed. He likes nothing more than to discuss philosophy with his guests. His wife and two young daughters live in Quito. It's the only way the children can get a good education. They visit him or he visits them on weekends.

That first night at the hacienda I suffered an upset stomach and had a bad case of insomnia. When morning arrived I was exhausted, but we prepared to hike up to the Ilinizas refugio anyway. Rodrigo told us how to get to the dirt road that led up towards the refugio. His directions were as follows: "Go up the dirt road passing by the hacienda, take the first right; then take the first left and walk up to a gate. Go through the gate and continue up the field all the way to a corner formed by pines, enter the pines and cross a small gully, then take another right, which leads to the road." Rodrigo also reminded us to look back occasionally. "Always look for the bright red roof of the hacienda," he said.

We left right after breakfast about 8 a.m. When we passed through the gate and approached the pines we couldn't see where they formed anything that resembled a corner, so we just followed what looked like a trail heading up through them.

When we came across what appeared to be a road we followed it to the bottom of a huge gully. Something didn't seem right but we proceeded to walk along the small stream that flowed through the gully anyway. We were soon stopped dead in our tracks by a wall of dense tangled vegetation, and ankle deep mud and water.

We returned to where the road had ended and David decided to check what looked like another trail leading downstream. I waited to see if he was going to get anywhere. He soon hollered for me to follow. Like a fool I did.

When the so-called trail petered out, David had ascended the near vertical and jungle-like wall of the gully. The vegetation was so thick it was extremely difficult to proceed. I had trekking poles but I really needed a machete. One of the poles hung up on the vegetation and broke in two. I almost fell. Foul language echoed down the gully when I grabbed for a clump of long wet grass and it proceeded to slice my fingers. I was lucky the grass held my weight. If it hadn't, I would've tumbled at least 60 feet back down to the spongy stream bottom.

After gaining a few more feet I saw something-vibrant green in color with black spots move under the grass just before placing my hand down. I was really relieved when it moved again and saw it was only a frog and not a snake. Later back at the hacienda, I learned from one of Rodrigo's books that it was a species of frog that exudes a poison through its skin.

David, able to fully recover from his ordeal, was laughing when I finally emerged at the top of the gully. I was more than a little upset. The detour cost us at least a half an hour, we got soaked by the vegetation and wasted lots of energy. I was even more upset later when from high above up on the dirt road we could clearly see that the lower part of the road crossed the gully where we were supposed to have gone. On our way back we only had to cross a six-foot deep ditch to get to where the pines formed a corner.

Each drink of water hit my stomach like a bomb as we continued to hike up the road towards the refugio. I blew it off as just a mild case of altitude sickness. I soon started to drag and David charged ahead. Every so often he waited for the feeble old man to catch up.

At the road's end we mistakenly followed a wide trail to the left instead of taking a right on what appeared to be a less traveled path. The well-worn trail we followed contoured around a long slope leading away from the refugio.

Nearing 14,000 feet we saw several bulls standing in the path just above us. The bulls roaming the high fields are the same ones trained locally for fighting. We decided not to push our luck and turned around. Back to where we had left the end of the road we discovered our error.

That evening after dinner a Safari Tours jeep dropped off John Race of Northwest Mountain Guides and his five American clients. They were going up to the refugio on Wednesday and planned to ascend Iliniza Norte on Thursday.

Later that night the path to the bathroom became familiar to me even in the dark. I was sick for the next two days. Since I was incapacitated, David decided to go to the refugio with the others to spend the night at the higher altitude.

For the next two days I took Cipro, an antibiotic guaranteed to cure "Tourisimo." I also drank gallons of tea and read every travel book Rodrigo had on Ecuador.

My partner returned from the refugio early Thursday afternoon. He had started out on his own up Iliniza Norte in the morning, but decided to turn back before it got to late. Race took two of his five clients to the summit. The other three weren't feeling up to it and remained behind in the refugio.

I was feeling better. But I wasn't looking forward to heading up to the Jose Ribas Refugio on Cotopaxi to spend the night at 15,477 feet. Our transportation arrived about 3 p.m., and the jeep driver proceeded to inform us that he had to wait for an American couple to arrive from the Ilinizas refugio. We waited for a half-hour. They never materialized.

The driver apologized to us and explained that the entrance gate to the one road leading into Cotopaxi National Park is closed and locked at 4 p.m. David was disappointed. I was relieved. Another night at Rodrigo's would only help me recover more fully.

The Northwest Mountain group was long overdue. The jeep driver decided he could make some money by driving up to meet them. It was probably his plan all along. He could communicate by cell phone with the hut guardian who knew the group was in bad shape. He found the six of them stumbling down in the near dark near the upper end of the road. One of Race's clients was seriously ill and could barely walk. Except for Race, who had his hands full, the entire group was wasted.

That night, Race had the jeep driver take him and one of his sick client's to a hospital in Quito. We learned later that the man had a bad case of food poisoning.

Friday morning our ride to Cotopaxi National Park arrived an hour early. We said our good-byes to Rodrigo and jumped aboard. On our way to the park we passed through the little highland community of La Comuna and drove by the Bull Tentadero "El Carmen" -- the local ring where some of the bulls we saw below the Ilinizas would likely meet their fate. The scenery was gorgeous, but clouds prevented us from getting a distant view of Cotopaxi.

A short drive on the Pan-American took us to the turnoff to Cotopaxi National Park. Just off the highway we drove by what looked like a shantytown. Then we traveled on a rough road through a strip-mined area. After passing through the park's gate we began to gain elevation on an improved dirt road. Woods along the sides of the road showed signs of past lumbering and heavy grazing.

Above the woods we drove for several more miles through the desolate brown and red arid plains below Cotopaxi. We passed by Ruminahui (15,460 feet), another extinct volcano in the park. We also drove past Laguna Limpiopungo, a large Andean lake at approximately 12,468 feet above sea level. Finally, we were dropped off at the parking lot about a 1/4-mile below the Jose Ribas Refugio.

Cotopaxi greeted us with clouds, sleet, and 40 to 50 mph winds. Meanwhile, a school bus pulled up and a large group of Ecuadorian teenagers piled out. None of them were dressed appropriately for the weather. They wore blue jeans, light jackets, and tennis shoes. I was very surprised when they proceeded to charge up the trail leading up to the refugio. Thirteen non-climbers perished last May, when an avalanche caught them standing around outside the building.

The refugio is a large solid two-story building. There were many other climbers inside when we arrived. We shared the upstairs sleeping quarters with a Spanish couple, a couple from Germany with an Ecuadorian Guide, two other Ecuadorian Guides and the group of American doctors they were shepherding.

We ate, and after organizing our equipment, crawled into our sleeping bags at 6 p.m. We set our alarms for 11:30 p.m.

It was just after midnight when we left the refugio. The weather was heinous. Cloud obscured the long moderate snow slopes and short steep icy ramps above us. And the mist, propelled by sustained 50-mph winds, was freezing on impact. Gambling that the conditions would improve later in the day higher up on the volcano, we headed off into the gloom. There were windows of better weather with more terrible weather in between as we slowly fought our way upward.

The ferocious wind absorbed the sound of our passage, as we passed by ice caves draped with enormous tropical icicles, carefully skirted numerous large crevasses, and nervously belayed each other across a number of sketchy looking snow bridges. Our headlamps and glasses glazed over and there were times that I could barely make out

David's footprints directly in front of my own two cramponed feet.

David continued to lead the way and just moved to where he thought the route went, hoping to see signs of where the others had passed before us and where snow bridges had been previously crossed.

My thoughts wavered from absolute confidence to hopeless anxiety. The doubt began to drain my strength and I had to feed off of my younger partner's energy to continue. Tethered together, I went where he went. And at times an urge to flee back down the volcano's treacherous slopes became overwhelming. But each time I hesitated the frozen cord connecting us came taut, and a slight tug on my waist kept prodding me to follow to where it led. Step by breathless step we continued onward and upward into the blowing tempest.

Finally near the 18,000 foot level and adjacent to the 400-foot rock wall called Yanasacha, which means "black wild place" in Quechua, it began to look like our wager on the weather was going to pay off. The sky began to clear. We could actually see the full moon and a slender sliver of the fiery orange sun rising on the far horizon.

Convinced the worst was over we moved onward with a renewed determination. Then, Cotopaxi upped the ante. The wind intensified and the temperature began to drop precipitously.

The fingers of my right hand wrapped around the metal of my ice axe started to freeze. I had to stop and put on a thicker pair of gloves beneath my Gore-Tex shell mittens. In the meantime, heavy black clouds engulfed us.

We climbed another thirty feet and then David halted to belay me up to him. It was difficult to tell, but I estimated that we were on a slope of about 50 degrees. Huddling together in order to hear each other over the savage wind David wanted to descend. Uncharacteristically, I pushed him to continue on for just one more rope length hoping against hope the weather would once again improve. One hundred and twenty feet higher we mutually agreed to descend. It wasn't a difficult decision to make. We knew there would be no view at the top, and I was running out of wands (thin four foot long plastic shafts with a bright orange flag attached to one end) to mark our route for a safe return.

I immediately began to retrace our steps. Lower down, the visibility gradually improved and I remember being amazed by the number of crevasses we had passed by on the way up in the dark. One snow bridge in particular occupied my mind since we had crossed it while ascending. It was about four feet wide and bridged a house-sized chasm. I kept wondering had it weakened? If it failed beneath one of us would the other be able to hold the fall? Would the unfortunate victim dangling inside the natural refrigerator be able to extricate himself? The two wands I had placed to identify its location suddenly appeared out of the gray mist. I pulled them out of the snow and placed them inside the compression straps on the left side of my pack. One slid through all three straps and raced down the icy slope at an astonishing speed. I followed its path with my eyes until it vanished into the black abyss of the crevasse. Was it an omen?

I waited apprehensively for David to ready a boot axe belay. Then suppressing my fear I took a very tenuous first step when he signaled for me to proceed. When I took another a very loud whomp startled me as the bridge settled beneath my weight. Expecting the worst I turned and looked back at David. Nothing happened. Then I slowly spread my legs apart to better distribute my weight but I couldn't control myself. I almost sprinted the rest of the way across.

Now, it was David's turn. He stepped in my steps. My dread wasn't replaced with relief until he made it safely across and stood beside me. We both relaxed; knowing the rest of the descent should be a breeze.

When we reached the lower glacier the warmth of the early morning had thawed the firm crust on top of the snow. We sank several feet into the soft and wet snow pack with each step the rest of the way back to the refugio. Twice, I toppled over when I sank up to my crotch.

It was only 8 a.m. when we arrived back at the refugio. Everybody else on the mountain soon joined us. Nobody had set foot on the summit, including the guided groups.

We had arranged to be picked up at 3 p.m. We teamed up with the Spanish couple and called to see if we could be picked up earlier and were told to be at the parking lot by 1 p.m.

After eating a snack the four of us packed our things and sat in the cold empty refugio until 12:30 p.m. All of the others had their own transportation and had already left for the parking lot.

Cotopaxi gave us a parting shot after we arrived at the parking lot. While waiting for our ride to appear we were assaulted by more high winds and a cold downpour. Our ride was an hour late.

We parted company with the Spanish couple in Lasso. They were headed south on a bus to Banos. David and I had made reservations to stay at the nearby Hosteria La Cienaga. It's a well-known retreat most climbers coming off of one of the high volcanoes spend some time at to recuperate. The former mansion is 400 years old and belongs to the Lasso Family, who once owned all of the land between Quito and Ambato some 85 miles to the south.

The entrance to the hosteria reminded me of the southern mansion in the movie "Gone with the Wind." Hundred foot high Eucalyptus trees border the quarter mile drive leading to the main building. Inside the hosteria, a flower-filled courtyard includes a large ornate fountain and chapel. Our room was enormous. It cost us $42.

We were a little underdressed for dinner, which probably accounted for our waiter's snobby behavior. I ordered the prawns. They were the largest I have ever seen. Our only complaint about the hosteria is that the bar only stocks the more expensive premium beer called Club. Pilsner, which is the cheaper local beer, has a far superior taste.

That evening in the hallway just outside our room we crossed paths with the Northwest Mountain group. They had arrived the day before. Everyone in the group seemed healthy except for one woman. The six of them planned to go to Cotopaxi in the morning. David got summit fever again and decided to join them. I wasn't interested in facing more lousy weather.

Sunday morning after breakfast they gave me a lift out to the Pan-American, where I caught the third bus to Quito that passed by. The first two were full. I got off the bus before it pulled into the main bus station in Old Town at a corner, where two cabs were waiting. First, I tried to get a bed at the Magic Bean, but they were full. I then tried two other nearby hotels before finding a room at the Hotel Embassy for $32.

That night I watched the news and the movie, "Thelma and Louise," on TV in Spanish. Monday morning, I had a great breakfast at the Cafe Cultura with a British chap, who was headed for Peru to hike the Inca Trail. After breakfast I went shopping for some souvenirs.

I checked into the Magic Bean about 12:30 p.m. When David arrived that afternoon he found me sitting under the covered terrace sipping a pilsner, writing postcards and talking to a young American. She was supporting herself, like so many others we had met while in Ecuador, by teaching English.

David informed me that he and the Northwest group never left the refugio that morning because of high winds. He also said that he had to help fix a flat on the Land Rover that delivered him back to Quito. I was pleased to hear that I had made the right choice after all.

We spent the rest of the day shopping for souvenirs, and that night we drank Scottish beers at the American/British-owned bar called, "La Reina Victoria." It was a fitting end to our latest adventure. Thanks to President Clinton, our American Airlines flight to Miami in the morning left right on time.

TREKKING THE VAL D' ASOTA

The Aosta Valley is located in the northwest corner of Italy and shares much of its northern border with Switzerland and its northwestern and western border with France.

The *Alta Via 4 is* a rugged footpath that passes from valley to valley over high passes in the heart of the mountains and close to the glaciers within the region of *Val d' Aosta*. Mountain huts (*rifugi* in Italian) are strategically located along the route, but even Italian walkers rarely do the entire walk from end-to-end. Completing the trek is a demanding undertaking that involves having to ascend and descend a total of almost 70,000 feet over a distance of 110 miles. The trail is generally well marked with triangles or slashes of yellow paint on boulders and cliff sides along the way, but route finding skills are essential. There are also four short but difficult and exposed sections where fixed protection such as iron ladder rungs and/or a cable or chains (called *via ferrata*) have been placed to help ensure safe passage or ascent.

The *Alta Via 4* begins in the tiny alpine village of Champorcher and ends at the foot of Mont Blanc on the streets of the lovely medieval city of Courmayeur. The route traverses Italy's spectacular and unspoiled Gran Paradiso National Park. The park was first created as a preserve in 1821 to protect one of the largest mammals indigenous to the Alps, the alpine ibex (whose name in Italian is *stembecco*). Ibex are not particularly afraid of humans and were almost hunted to extinction. Now thanks to the protection they receive within the park's borders, the majestic animals have become more plentiful and have been restocked to other areas throughout the Alps.

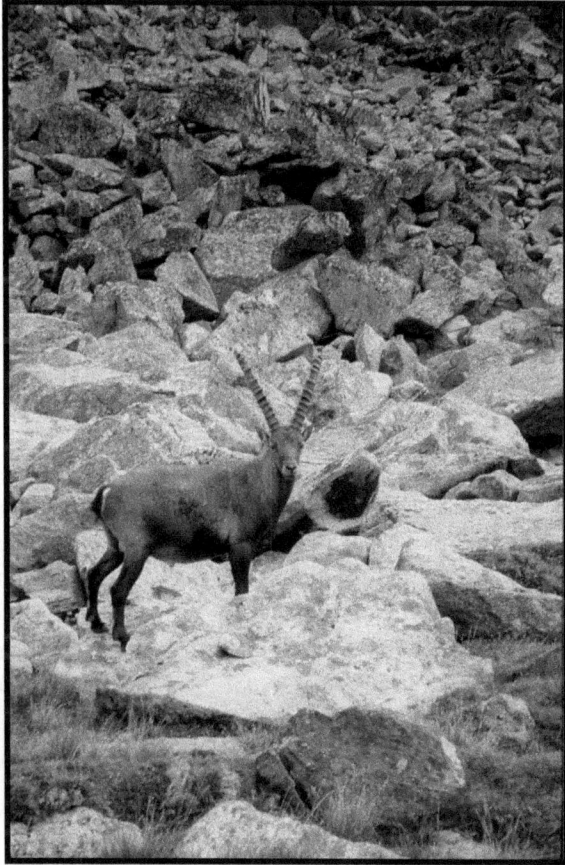

Ibex (Stembacco). (Photo by author)

David Panofsky, his wife, Pat Smith, and Christopher Celi, a graduate student at the University of Wisconsin, and I were attracted to the walk because the valleys of the Italian Alps are wilder and more wooded than their Swiss counterparts and less disfigured by skiing development than those in France. Once the main roads are left behind you can feel transported back a century to an era when the pace of life was solely connected to the demands of the land. The folk of the *Val d' Aosta* retain French as an important language, keeping faith to the time when the region was part of the duke of Savoy, and few of them have acquired the hard-nosed commercial mentality that has beset many other areas of the Alps.

Christopher had flown to Rome to visit relative's two weeks before we planned to begin the trek. David and Pat also flew over to the Continent early so they could spend some time with David's relatives. When I arrived in Milan on August 27th, the two of them were waiting for me at the airport with Gianna's car.

David's mother, Gianna Sommi, owns an apartment in Parma. After a day of rest at her apartment, David drove us to Entréves, a small village located just above Courmayeur. The four hour ride was uneventful except for the occasional motorcycle screaming by at over 120 mph, the few rude gestures aimed at David from other crazed drivers, and being pulled over by machine gun-toting Carabinieri for a "routine" document check.

In Entréves, we stayed at the Hotel Aiguille Noire where Mont Blanc, the highest point in the Alps (15,777 feet) towers directly over the village. David and I had planned to climb it after completing the trek. However, the weather that summer had been the warmest on record in the Alps. As a result, glaciers throughout the region were in poor climbing condition. Due to risk of ice and rock fall and the dangers associated with negotiating crevasses that were widening by the day, even the professional mountain guides of Courmayeur were telling everyone that all routes from the Italian side of Mont Blanc were in their opinion *"molto pericoloso"* (very dangerous).

The next morning, the four of us left by bus to travel back down the main valley to the city of Aosta and eventually on up to Champorcher. Four buses later, we arrived in Champorcher and hit the trail. It was a three-hour up hill jaunt to our first destination; the mountain hut called Rufugio Dondena.

David had made advance reservations for each night of the trek. In fact, he had scheduled the entire trip so carefully that it was rare for us to need more than a few minutes to plan the next day. We had hoped to be able to complete the entire walk back to Courmayeur in 11 days. After the first day, to keep to our schedule we needed to average six to eight hours of hiking each day.

On the second (and first full) day of our trek, we decided to split up. Christopher and I followed a somewhat easier section of another high route called the *Alta Via 2*, while David and Pat stayed true to the *Alta Via 4*.

We planned to meet up that afternoon in the village of Cogne.

On top of the Finestra di Champorcher (a high pass), Christopher and I had a fine view of the Gran Paradiso, which at 13,320 feet is the highest peak wholly within Italy, and La Grivola, a challenging 13,018-foot objective for climbers. The rest of that day's hike for the two of us mostly involved a grueling 4,395-foot descent down the Val Urtier to Lillaz, the last village at the end of the Valle di Cogne.

Meanwhile, David and Pat had to first hike up to the Colle di Pontonnet, where in addition to our view they had an excellent view of two peaks of the nearby Monte Rosa group on the Italian-Swiss border. They then had to descend a section of trail before having to re-ascend to a second pass called the Col des Hevergnes. From the second pass, they also had to suffer a punishing and very long, steep descent through the wilder Val Grauson.

Christopher and I arrived in Cogne sore and tired an hour ahead of them. When the four of us met in the town's main square we had two things on our minds: *gelato* (Italian for ice cream) and cold beer.

The following day, we hiked from the Hotel Herbetet up the Valle di Valnontey along the Torrente Valnontey to a small wooden bridge that provides access over the turbulent river. We then climbed very steep switchbacks up the north side of the narrow valley to a grassy hillside that overlooks the Gran Paradiso, its icefalls, and numerous waterfalls plunging to the river far below.

We paused for lunch and then proceeded on a long and relatively exposed traverse to the Pian di Resello. The high platform is approximately 2,870 feet above Cogne and provides a good view up the Val Urtier, which Christopher and I had descended the day before.

Eventually, the trail becomes very narrow and increasingly exposed. Then it widens to the size of a mule track near the Laghetto del Lauson. After passing the small lake, the trail gently descends to the Rifugio Vittorio Sella, a large and popular hut located in a wide meadow at 8,476 feet. The lush meadow, which is divided by a slow moving stream, is frequently filled in the evenings and early mornings with ibex and chamois -- a smaller and more graceful goat-like alpine species with short black horns.

On the fourth day of the trek, we had to complete the longest and most difficult section of the route. It involves crossing two passes over 10,800 feet high and climbing a steep (300 foot high) rock face.

We made short order of the first pass even though near its top the trail was very steep and the footing became rather greasy. The path on the other side descends even more steeply and passes below the somber wall of the Punta Bianca until it enters a second valley lower in elevation than the Rif. V. Sella. At that point the trail meanders along fairly level terrain for a couple of miles before making a traverse up into another valley. While making the uphill traverse, we rounded a sharp bend and came upon two large stone chalets and a number of ibex. We decided to stop there for lunch and our wild audience wearily watched our every move.

After eating, we descended to a large boulder field and searched out a dry passage over many separate channels of the Torrente Leviona. When we re-located the trail on the other side of the rushing waters, we had to climb straight up one of the largest glacial moraines I've ever seen. The trail travels atop the lateral moraine's crest to near its summit where it then steeply descends to a broken shelf of rock and seemingly disappears near a shallow cascade that flows across the rock shelf. I walked through the swift water and, eventually picked up a yellow splash of paint above us on a large boulder. From there a faint trail continued to ascend the very broken melt-out debris immediately adjacent to the crevasse riddled Gran Neyron glacier. We soon found ourselves on scree mixed with ice and realized we were actually on the glacier.

Finally, we reached the base of the vertical rock face we had to climb to reach a notch, which is hidden from below and is called the Colle del Gran Neyron. Christopher had very limited experience in the mountains and had worried about this section. I led the way, Pat followed me, and behind her, David assisted Christopher. As it turned out, the part of the trek Christopher most feared was the part he enjoyed the most.

The views from the pass that afternoon were indescribable: the minarets on the sculpted ridge leading to the summit of Herbetet; the rugged, almost fairy-tale looking Becca di Montandayné; and the dirty looking blanket of the Montandayné glacier. We all felt distinctly privileged that momentarily we had such a wonderful place to ourselves and our moods improved dramatically. Even when it started to rain shortly after we descended from the airy perch, our spirits weren't dampened. We just quickly donned our Gore-Tex parkas and plodded on.

Fourteen hours after starting out that morning, we finally arrived at the Rifugio Chabod where we were crammed into a tiny room. That evening we celebrated our day's accomplishment and David and Pat's third anniversary.

In the morning Pat woke up to three different watch alarms. She accused us guys of trying to drive her mad. We were totally fogged in all through breakfast and a hard rain continued to fall.

After much discussion on whether we should move on or stay put, we agreed to cut our scheduled hike for the day in half and try to find a place to stay in Pont, a small hamlet at the very end of the road in the Val Savarenche.

The depressing weather lifted by the time we reached our destination. We also got lucky and were able to get two rooms at the only hotel in town (the Hotel Paradiso) at cheap off-season rates. We used the needed time off from walking to wash our extra clothing and to write a few postcards.

The downside of our unscheduled stop was that when we called ahead to inform the rest of the rifugios that we'd be a day late, we learned that a hut in France and all nearby alternatives would be closing for the season. This caused us to re-route through Italy, descending through the town of Valgrisenche to the little village of Planaval and up and over what an Italian guide had described to us as "an easy pass with a trivial glacier." Looking back on the ascent to the Colle di Planaval, it turned out to be our one encounter with the perils we'd heard and read about (i.e. the unusual and dangerous conditions that summer in the high Alps).

Our rest at the Hotel Paradiso felt like paradise and provided us with the psychological lift we needed before continuing our quest to complete the entire 110-mile long journey.

The next leg of the trek starts directly behind the hotel, where it steeply switchbacks up a cliff past a waterfall and on up to a large cross, which marks the end of a hanging valley, the Piano del Nivolet. Already almost 1,000 feet above Pont, the location of the cross provides a fine view across the Val Savarenche.

The morning was bright and clear. We could see the entire Gran Paradiso Massif and both of the high passes we had stood on two days ago. That afternoon, the fickle weather changed again, and as we approached the upper end of the hanging valley, thick clouds began to rapidly spill down its headwall.

We planned to spend the night at the Rifugio Citta di Chivasso, which is located at the head of the valley just below the Col Del Nivolet. It started to pour right after we stepped inside the small rustic shelter. The interior of the building seemed more suited to mountaineers than the previous

Refugio's we had stayed at. We had to ascend a ladder and pass through a trap door to reach our beds which were in an attic-like loft, and a headlamp is a necessity when having to use the facilities downstairs after dark.

The next morning, we were awakened by the dreaded tap-tap-tap of graupel (granular snow) dancing on our second story room's little window. We prolonged the standard breakfast of stale bread, jam, and strong coffee, and purposely stalled our start waiting for the weather to improve.

Christopher had to return to Milan in order to make his flight home. We said our good-byes to him outside in the rain.

When we parted company, he headed back to Pont to catch a bus to Aosta and the three of us left for the Col Rossett. Initially, Pat David and I took the wrong fork in the trail, but we soon realized our mistake and corrected it by traversing into the right valley. As we gained elevation, it began to snow. However, the pass was reasonable for us even in the foul weather.

On the opposite side of the pass, the clouds started to break apart. The lighting effect was quite dramatic each time a shaft of sunshine struck the surrounding peaks, which wore a new dusting of snow.

We descended to the small, boulder-strewn valley below and stopped for lunch. When we continued on our way, several rocks ahead of us began to move. We soon realized the mobile objects were chamois -- there appeared to have been more than 100 of them. As we approached closer, they gracefully bounded up the side slope above us and circled around behind us.

The trail eventually crosses over a small stream and ascends the steep slope on the opposite side of the valley before wrapping around a blind corner where the side valley enters the much larger Val di Rhêmes. When we made the turn we encountered one of the most impressive sights I've ever seen in the mountains. Directly in front of us, but at a distance, stood a massive mountain (the Granta Parei) with a sheer 1,000-ft. rock wall. Far below it we could also see our destination for that evening, the Rifugio Benevolo and, still farther down the valley, the longest and largest waterfall of the trip. The spectacular vista again affected our moods and turned what had begun as a foul, windy, wet and sleety somewhat miserable day into our second magical experience during the trek.

Pat Smith and David Panofsky trekking towards the Granta Parei.
(Photo by author)

It was an even wilder scene at the Rifugio. The building, which holds 80 people, was filled to capacity. Including many others, there was a contingent of geology professors on a field trip and a large and raucous group from the flatland town of Piacenza. The flatlanders were on their first alpine club outing and we had to share a room with 12 of them. They knew nothing about how to behave in cramped hut conditions. Fortunately for us, we had arrived first and claimed the third tier bunks on one side of the room where we were able to watch the pandemonium below us. When the lights finally went out, we stuffed our earplugs in as deep as possible.

The next morning dawned clear and chilly. We warmed up quickly as the trail climbed steadily upward to the beautiful Lago di Goletta. This glacial lake at the foot of the Goletta glacier is an impressive sight with the steep snout of the glacier plunging into its turquoise colored water.

We continued upward towards the Colle Bassac Deré. The ascent up to the high pass is very steep and over snow. The conditions, however, were perfect (no need for crampons) and we were soon at the top.

The view on the other side of the pass of the Italian wall of the Grande Sassiére complete with its own huge hanging glacier, and of the crevasses and patterns of the Gliairetta glacier below, was almost more amazing then the view from the side we had just ascended.

A very fit Italian couple in their 70s soon joined us. They were from Torino and visited the mountains every chance they got. We learned they were staying at the Rifugio Bezzi (our own destination for that evening). They invited us to join them on an ascent of the Becca Della Traversiere, where they planned to eat their lunch. I took their picture and they were off. A little later, we set out after them in hot pursuit.

When we reached a small hidden col, we could see the summit, which hadn't been in view before. I had left my parka in my pack back at the pass and when a cold wind picked up, I turned back. David and Pat made the 10,945-foot high point, which straddles the French-Italian border, a half-hour after I had left them.

When they returned to the pass, we descended to the Rifugio. The food at the Ref. Bezzi is well known throughout the region and it lived up to its reputation. For dinner that night, we were served excellent soup, semolina dumplings in béchamel sauce, baby carrots, frittata (omelet), salad, cheese, and a peach. We were even able to get separate rooms, which was a luxury from the night before.

On our ninth day of hiking, we descended from the Refugio to the town of Valgrisenche. That morning it drizzled, and then it rained hard, stopped, drizzled again, and finally began to pour just as we entered the small town. We found rooms above a smoky but friendly bar.

It was still pouring in the afternoon, and we tried to get a weather forecast and find someone that knows the glacier we were to cross the next day. Our guidebook advised hikers who plan to cross over the Col di Planaval to rent crampons and hire a guide. We only had in-step crampons with us, but considered ourselves experienced mountaineers.

The road was wet and the sky was still a leaden gray when we left early the next morning. Planaval sits above the main valley road clustered around its pale yellow colored church. We passed through the tiny village via a narrow alley built for the passage of livestock.

From Planaval, the route ascends a one lane dead-end road to where a path twists endlessly upwards. We shared the narrow trail with a number of cows and had to sidestep the many fresh gifts they left behind.

Eventually we came upon several stone chalets. Above the chalets, the trail disappears.

We struggled up the steep muddy banks of a small end moraine incised by a stream and Pat took a slight tumble. She was unhurt, but it made us pause and question if we were going the right way. The slope behind the moraine flattened out and, to increase its velocity, the stream had braided into numerous shallow channels.

Around a bend in the U-shaped valley, we got our first look at the Glacier du Planaval. Both our guidebook and map indicate that the route ascends the moraine along the glacier's north margin. The waves of ice descending towards us looked tame enough at that distance, but closer up it became clear that without the proper equipment it was going to be a very serious obstacle to overcome.

David is diabetic and he stopped to check his blood sugar. Pat waited for him and I moved on ahead to get a better look at the route leading up to the pass.

Up on top of the glacier's snout, I studied the so-called route with my binoculars. I could see that to ascend the moraine forming along the north margin of the ice, we'd have to pass beneath a slope of dangerously loose rocks and scramble up, through, and over some very large and potentially unstable debris that could shift at any moment. There were also some very ugly looking crevasses on both sides of the moraine.

As I stood there weighing the route's objective dangers, a rock fall thundered down onto the glacier from the other side of its cirque. The biggest rock (the size of a small car) slid along like a bulldozer until it wedged into an open crevasse. It was a clear demonstration of the serious risk we faced being on the glacier in the heat of the day.

Still if we wished to continue the haphazard soil and rock piled along the glacier's north margin was the only feasible line to take. If we'd had our full crampons, rigid climbing boots, rope and ice axes; we could have ascended the exposed ice directly.

David and Pat began yelling at me to come back and I tried to encourage them to join me. "Come on!" I shouted and motioned with my arm for them to come. "It's no problem."

They weren't moving, so I reluctantly descended back down to them. "I think we should go back," David had said. "It's way too dangerous."

He had just broken a strap on one of his in-step crampons. Luckily, he was able to fashion a way to attach the crampon to his boot because there was no way I was going to descend the 4,375 feet down to the main road below Planaval. From there we'd then have to take a 50-mile bus ride back down to Asota and on up the next valley to ski resort of La Thuile. Fortunately, I was able to convince both of them to at least go up to where

I'd been to take a look.

Water was flowing over the lower section of the glacier and it was covered with every imaginable size and shape of debris so typical of a shrinking ice sheet. When we reached the spot where I had studied the route, I just kept walking. Both of them assured me that I was crazy but they soon followed me.

Working together, we slowly moved up and through the jumbled mess of terrain. Each one of us worried about a different danger. Pat was afraid of slipping into a crevasse, and being wedged inside the bowels of the ice and ever so slowly freezing to death or possibly being sucked into a water-filled cavity. David was concerned about the surface debris and its unpredictable potential for collapsing on top of us. Meanwhile, I kept looking up expecting to see a guided missile falling from the shattered slope above us.

It was a difficult and exhilarating scramble. I almost lost my resolve to continue twice. The first time, my crampons failed to take purchase and I began to slip on a steep section of ice covered with saturated mud and gravel towards a crevasse. Stones that I had dislodged rolled into the abyss, and my crampons bit just in time to avoid my joining them. The second time, I had grabbed a large rock to hoist myself up through two enormous blocks sitting on top of the moraine. The rock I grabbed was loose and it toppled into my chest and arms. I was barely able to direct it to the side where it fell harmlessly into a crevasse filled with water. If it had hit my leg instead, it probably would have broken it or smashed my ankle. It also could have landed on Pat who was right below me. If something serious had happened to any of us, a rescue before nightfall would not have been possible.

We were immensely relieved when we reached the safety of the pass. It delivered us onto the vast and almost flat Rutor ice field where the sun reflected brightly off of the snow and ice, shadow betrayed hundreds of open crevasses, and the black pyramid-shaped Testa Del Rutor wore a summit cloud that flowed down towards Valgrisenche.

We followed the crest of the Rutor glacier's large marginal moraine, which stands 50 feet above the retreating ice. At the end of the moraine we descended to a rocky area that had been covered by the huge glacier in a former time, and a little lower down we came upon two lovely little tarns (glacial lakes). Before walking the rest of the way to the hut, we took a refreshing swim to celebrate still being alive.

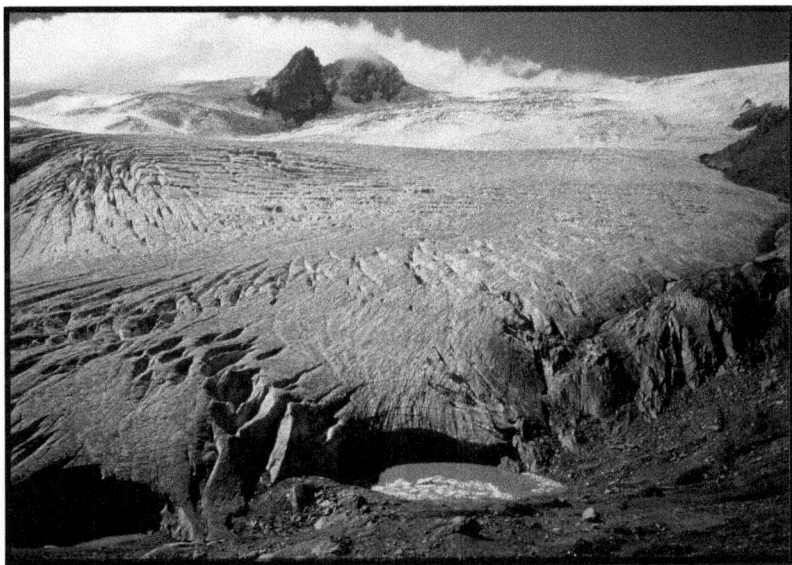

Rutor Glacier with the Testa Del Rutor in the background, and an iceberg filled tarn in the foreground. (Photo by author)

The Rif. Deffeyes custodian saw us coming and greeted us outside. "Bravo!" he exclaimed. "Bravo!" Apparently, we were the first party to risk the ascent from Planaval that season.

The next morning we quickly descended along the Rutor Torrente and by its three famous cascate (waterfalls) down to La Thuile, which was the biggest town we passed through on the trek.

From La Thuile, we had to follow a dirt road that never seemed to end up the monotonous Vallone di Chavannes to the Col di Chavannes. The pass consists of a bare knob of highly weathered shale and overlooks the Rifugio Elisabetta far below on the opposite side of the Val Veny on the lower slopes of Mont Blanc.

When we arrived at the hut it was filled with trekkers, who were circumnavigating the Mont Blanc Massif. The Tour of Mont Blanc (TMB) is a very popular long distance hike that parallels the lower slopes of the massif and travels over a number of passes allowing TMBer's to hike in France, Switzerland and Italy.

We had a great dinner that evening with a Swiss family of four, a former French guide who's now in his 90s, and two British blokes named

Rege and Dave. The following morning the two Brits joined us for most of the nondescript walk along a paved road into Courmayeur.

A heavy rain that night and a forecast for the storm to last for the next four days dashed any further climbing ambitions David or I had.

When we left for Parma in the morning, Pat suggested we take the train the next day from Parma to Venice. We spent two days in the extraordinary city of canals and "maze-like" streets and courtyards. I swore to return with Judy.

A lifelong friend of David's invited us to dinner the night before we were scheduled to leave Parma. I had lost nine pounds on the trek. During that evening I had to loosen my belt after consuming portions of four different types of homemade, stuffed pastas and various other dishes, desserts and liqueurs at the Famiglia Benedetti's place.

GUIDE TRAINING

assan Mossanen, a mountain guide originally from Iran, teased me from above as I dangled from my waist harness 30 feet below the surface of the Kahiltna Glacier. Enthralled by the beauty of the cobalt blue cavity in the ice, I hesitated to begin the procedures for self-rescue. Puzzled by my lack of motion Sassan's taunting turned to alarm and, he shouted, "Paul! Are you all right?" I nonchalantly replied, "I'm fine. I'm just admiring the view." Reminded by his genuine concern that in a real crevasse fall I knew that I'd be extremely anxious to get back to the surface, I swung into action.

Careful not to drop it, I tied a figure-eight knot in the middle of a long piece of 6mm cord to create a large loop, fixed it to the taut rope holding me from above by wrapping it around the rope to form a prussik knot, and attached one end of the cord to a locking carabiner on my harness. I then placed my right foot in a smaller loop I'd made previously in the free end of the cord to stand up and take the weight off of my harness. Finally, I clamped an ascender that was already connected to my harness by a nylon sling and another locking carabiner onto the rope above the prussik knot and slowly ascended my lifeline back to the glacier's surface.

My usual climbing partner, David Panofsky, had his hands full helping to organize an all-diabetic climb of Cerro Aconcagua, the highest mountain in the Western Hemisphere (see web page *www.Idea2000.org* for details). Therefore, I applied to take the Mountain Guide Course

Leaving crevasse rescue practice area. (Photo by author)

offered by the Alaska Mountaineering School. The unique non-profit school founded by Caitlin Palmer and Colby Coombs is located in Talkeetna, Alaska. At only 300 feet above sea level, the small Alaskan outpost is the destination and staging area for climbers aspiring to ascend the highest peak in North America, 20,320-foot high Mt. McKinley (Denali) and other peaks within the Alaska Range.

Information provided by the school indicated that snowshoes would be used as the mode of travel. I've never skied so you can imagine my surprise and concern when Colby greeted me at the doorstep of the school's little red log cabin with, "Hey Paul! Glad to see yea made it. Get your boots out so we can fit'em to skis." I stammered, "But I don't ski." He just chuckled and replied, "You do now."

My confidence took another hit when Caitlin introduced me to the other two students taking the course - Veli-Pekka Molsa and W. Hugh Gaasch. Veli-Pekka, who we all fondly just called VP, is a Finnish Airborne Ranger, who had competed in the 1999 "Eco-Challenge" held in Patagonia. His team of four finished the extreme endurance race in 14th place. Hugh had taken the advanced mountaineering course offered by the Alaska Mountaineering School the previous year. At that time, he also had 25 years of winter camping, skiing, and climbing experience already under his belt.

Besides Colby, two other instructors (Sassan, and Johnny Soderstrom, a 21-year-old Alaskan native) joined us on the course. At 54, I was old enough to be the entire group's father.

Talkeetna Air Taxi airlifted the six of us in two Cessna 185s to the famous airstrip and Denali Base Camp located at an elevation of 7,200 feet on the East Fork of the Kahiltna Glacier. It's the only location on the glacier where your next step isn't likely to send you plunging deep inside a bottomless crevasse.

After unloading the two planes, we placed extra gear and supplies into plastic sleds, clipped on our skis, donned our heavy packs, roped up into two teams of three and moved about 100 yards up slope away from the crowd. Before untying from our ropes and beginning the chore of setting up camp, Colby probed the area in a grid pattern for crevasses with a 20-foot collapsible aluminum rod. Johnny then delineated the perimeter of the "safe area" with wands.

We had four shovels and it still took us over an hour to excavate and pack down platforms for our two tents, construct a kitchen area, and build protective walls of snow around the tents and kitchen to protect us from storms. Before cooking dinner we staked down anything left outside our tents to prevent it from blowing away and marked where each item was with a wand so we'd be able to find it in the morning if it should snow overnight.

Colby designed the Mountain Guide Course to meet the stringent criteria of the American Mountain Guide's Association. The 14-day course moves through a progression that becomes more difficult and challenging each day.

Our first morning we practiced placing and testing the strength of several different types of snow anchors. Burying a picket horizontally in a trench and backed up by a couple of other pickets provided the most security in the loose snow.

Afterwards we roped up into two teams of three and skied up glacier directly across from the awesome snow and ice-covered buttresses and dangerous hanging glaciers and seracs of 14,500-foot Mt. Hunter.

When we turned around Colby directed me to take the lead and to choose a new route rather than just follow our tracks back to camp. While tentatively skiing around the obvious open crevasses I was ever aware that underneath the snow lurked numerous gaping cracks that could potentially swallow me whole. A sense of tension more than fear developed inside my gut and it only dissipated when we were back safe within the confines of our probed campsite.

The next day we returned to the same area to practice crevasse rescue. After Colby found a suitable opening in the ice and probed and wanded a safe area for us to congregate in, he instructed the three of us students to install a snow belay/anchor system that we'd trust our lives to.

When everybody was finally satisfied with our anchor, Sassan and Colby demonstrated how to set up different pulley systems for extracting a climber from a crevasse. The rest of us took turns setting up each system and playing the victim by being lowered into the icy slot to practice self-rescue as described earlier.

We broke camp the following morning and began skiing down glacier. The Kahiltna has an average width of about two miles and it's the longest glacier (about 45 miles in length) in the Alaska Range. Our destination was a tributary to the Kahiltna 24 miles to the south called the Pika Glacier. Again roped together in two teams of three, we were able to travel an average of six miles a day while carrying 50 lb. packs and pulling 40 lb. sleds.

Hugh Gassch packed up, roped in, and ready to rock and roll.
(Photo by author)

Skiing roped together past Mt. Foraker. (Photo by author)

During the first full day of travel I remember asking myself over and over, "What the hell did I get myself into?" When we finally stopped for the day, I found that I had developed blisters on the end of all of my toes and I just wanted to go home.

From that day on, each one of us took a turn being "Leader for the Day." As the leader we were responsible for making all major decisions such as what time to get under way, picking the safest and most expeditious route, when to take a break, where to camp for the night, and who should do which chores such as building a latrine, logging the weather etc. My turn came on the day we skied down and around the glacier's Icefall. It was the only day we were able to remove the nylon skins from our skis, which allowed us to travel uphill over the undulating glacier, and use wax instead. I surprised myself and only fell once when I picked up too much speed and tried to slow down.

Colby constantly emphasized speed and proficiency in performing every task. A rest stop meant immediately dropping your pack to conserve energy and putting on or taking off a layer of clothing if you were too cold or hot, remembering to eat a quick snack to re-fuel and to guzzle a drink to avoid dehydration, and also to reapply sun block to prevent having your face and lips burn to a crisp. If you failed to complete any of these minor comforts, you simply suffered the consequences for another two hours until the next break.

The Alaska Range is well known for its cold, but few people are aware of the extreme heat a climber endures while on a glacier when the northern sun is shining. I've experienced the radiant power of the sun on high mountains in Mexico and South America, but nothing had prepared me for the heat on the Kahiltna. The ambient air temperatures ranged from lows of -20 to 16 degrees Fahrenheit at night, and they were only in the 30s by early afternoon. But the reflective snow and ice on the glacier acts like a giant oven, and we were forced to set up camp by 1:00 or 2:00 every day to avoid severe dehydration or getting heat stroke.

Johnny Soderstrom waits for Colby Coombs to probe for crevasses at new campsite. (Photo by author)

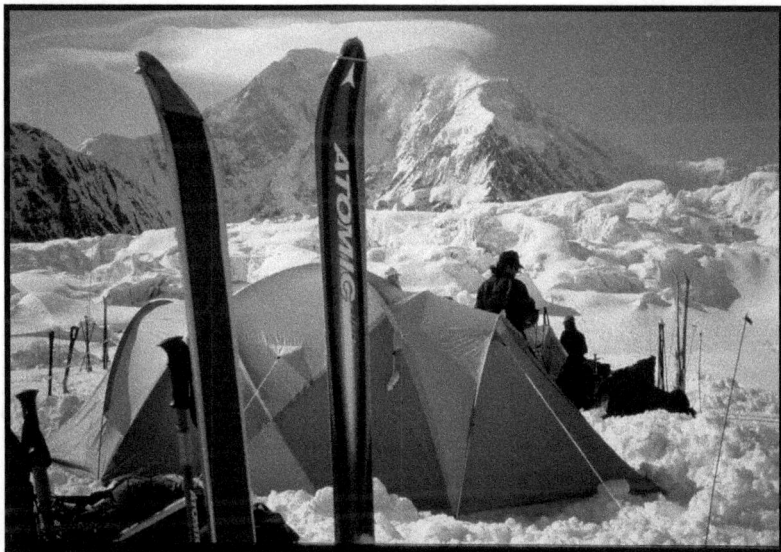

Campsite just below the Icefall. (Photo by author)

We stayed two nights at our third camp in order to make a first ascent of Peak 8020. Our route follows a beautiful 3000-foot long snow and ice covered ridge to the peak's previously virgin summit. The view from the top of the peak is both intimidating and indescribably beautiful. To the east it's filled with the steep and unstable slopes of Avalanche Spire. Off to the west, Mt. Russell stands above row upon row of rugged snow covered peaks. And, the three giants of the Alaska Range (Denali, 17,400-foot high Mt. Foraker, and Mt. Hunter) dominate the view to the north. We could even see the terminus of the Kahiltna to the south and miles upon miles of barren tundra beyond it. The pure, undiluted wilderness and tremendous space around us made me feel as if we were the only six humans on the planet.

Crossing huge filled crevasse, while descending Peak 8020.
(Photo by author)

We reached the base of the Pika's Icefall two days later. I ran out of water while ascending 1500 feet in elevation up the steep side glacier and really suffered. All I could do was put my head down, grit my teeth and go for it. I remember VP jokingly telling me, "Paul, there's an old Ranger saying. Pain is a sensation and sensations are to be enjoyed."

When we finally stopped for the day it was my turn to build the latrine. It took everything I had left to construct a well-protected throne with the prerequisite gorgeous view.

In the morning we loaded our extra food and fuel onto the sleds and cached them in a snow hole. We then set off to establish a camp up on a col high above an adjacent and even steeper Icefall. We soon had to remove our skis because one slip on the steep ice meant sliding into one of many very nasty-looking crevasses.

Author on the right ascending tributary glacier above Pika Glacier.
(Photo by Veli-Pekka Molsa)

After reaching the col, Johnny demonstrated how to saw and shape blocks of snow. The instructors then used the blocks to fortify their tent and the three of us students were told to excavate a snow cave. I quickly learned the value of having a pair of Neoprene gloves by nearly freezing my fingers while digging in the snow with wet liner gloves. It was a lot of work, but our cave was much warmer than a tent since snow is one of nature's best insulators. I actually had to crawl outside in the middle of the night to take off a layer of clothes.

The area around the Pika is called "Little Switzerland" because steep peaks of excellent granite surround the frozen river of ice.

Over the next two days we attempted to ascend Her Highness and successfully topped out on the Italian Boot. Our route up the almost perfect, pyramid-shaped peak named Her Highness was quite steep. It varied from 50-70 degrees and the condition of the snow was dramatically different from one spot to the next. One minute we'd be casually kicking steps or be cramponing on top of a hard crust, the next moment we'd be wallowing through unstable thigh-deep snow hoping to gain any purchase possible and worrying about setting off an avalanche.

147

Colby found the snow conditions nearer her summit to be so unstable that he decided not to risk bringing the rest of us any further up the mountain. We bagged the climb then and there and returned to camp.

On our way back Colby decided to set up a top rope on a large exposed vertical face of glacial ice just above our camp and we all had fun taking turns practicing our ice climbing skills.

On our last day to climb and after descending from the summit of the Italian Boot and returning to our high camp our instructors returned to the Pika and left us to fend for ourselves. We took our time breaking camp before heading back down through the crevasse-riddled Icefall. Roped together we moved confidently as one. And upon reaching the relative safety of the Pika where the instructors were waiting for us, VP passed around a small flask of Finnish Schnapps to celebrate our graduation so to speak.

We established our last camp on a large level area further up the Pika. The next day we practiced locating buried avalanche transceivers and various rappelling procedures that can be used to rescue an injured or even unconscious climber.

Our run of perfect weather was ending and we weren't at all sure all six of us would be able to return to Talkeetna in the morning. But the second flight brought the three left behind home well before dark. Caitlin and Colby put on a big feed at the school (barbecued King Salmon, caribou and moose burgers, vegetarian chili, rice and fresh garden salad). The students bought the beer.

The last official day of the course was spent inside the Talkeetna Ranger Station listening to the lecture and watching the slide show given to climbers who register to climb Denali or Mt. Foraker. The National Park Service wants to impress upon the climbers what awaits them out there and make sure they at least have the proper equipment to survive the unforgiving polar environment. The slide show includes lots of gruesome pictures of frostbite injuries, body recoveries, etc.

While we'd enjoyed incredibly clear and relatively calm weather awesome-looking lenticular clouds formed on top of both Denali and Mt. Foraker almost every day. Once when we had radio communication with the 11,000-foot camp on Denali, we were told the encampment was experiencing temperatures of 40 degrees below zero and winds of 80 mph.

Ascending Her Highness. (Photo by author)

Before receiving our diploma, Colby asked us to evaluate the course. I wrote that it was brutal, but I also advised him not to change a thing. Over the past 15 years, I have taught many people to climb and have done a little guiding, but I learned a ton. I also now know from first-hand experience what's meant by the term "Alaska Factor" that climbers use to describe the difficulty of climbing in the Frontier State. It stands for "Everything is farther away than it looks, harder than it looks, and will take longer than you think it will."

THIRD TIME WASN'T THE CHARM

O
n my third visit to the mountains and glaciers of Alaska, my goal was to climb Mt. Bona, which at 16,421 feet is the highest peak in the Wrangell Mountains. The remote and snowy mountain is an old stratovolcano located in the largest unit in our national park system, the Wrangell – St. Elias National Park and Preserve. The park is six times the size of Yellowstone and abuts against Glacier Bay National Park to the south and shares its eastern border with Canada's Kluane National Park. The three parks combined, encompass a whopping 42 million acres of pristine wilderness that holds most of the highest mountains in North America and contains glaciers and ice fields that are some of the largest outside of the Polar Regions. The entire area is designated as a UN World Heritage Site.

Recently retired and nearing my 56th birthday, I'd never worked as hard to get in shape for a climb. Then a month before leaving for Alaska a foreboding began to erode my enthusiasm. While I had to fly from Milwaukee to Atlanta to make a connection to Anchorage and would need to take two bush plane flights to reach a very remote Base Camp, my anxiety was due to more than just flying after 9/11. My family even sensed my hesitation, and I scared my wife Judy by discussing the pertinent details of my life insurance policies. I'd never broached the subject with her before leaving on many other climbing trips and expeditions. My attitude deteriorated when right before my scheduled departure of June 1, two mountaineering accidents (one on Mt. Rainier and other on Mt. Hood), involving the deaths of six climbers and a spectacular helicopter crash, were being sensationalized on the local and national news.

Unlike the incredibly clear and calm weather I had experienced while in the Alaska Range two years previously, I was met at the Anchorage airport by gray skies and a cold drizzle. The gloomy conditions just reminded me that the Wrangell Mountains and St. Elias Range are noted for weather as bad as anywhere on earth.

An Inupiat cabbie dropped me off at the Parkwood Inn where I was to rendezvous with the rest of the team put together by the Alaska Mountaineering and Climbing School. After checking in, I met head guide Sean Gaffney and his two assistant guides, Mike "Cedar" DuMont and

Eric Raikko. Eric followed me up to my room and checked my personal gear. I then repacked, showered, and at 2 a.m. Alaskan time tried to get a few hours of shuteye.

I met the other seven members of the team in the morning. We then loaded everything for the eleven of us (including three weeks of fuel and food for a little more than one week of climbing) into and on top of a large van and in Sean's pickup truck camper.

The sun was shining when we left to drive to Chitina - a tiny Alaskan airport consisting of a small trailer, two storage sheds, and a gravel airstrip on a fluvial terrace deposited by the Chitina River. When we approached the Matanuska Valley on the Glenn Highway, it clouded over and began to pour. The unwelcome precipitation didn't let up until we entered the town of Glennallen. It was threatening to rain again when we arrived in Chitina so we quickly unpacked the vehicles and covered everything with plastic tarps. When the rain resumed we stood under the eve of the largest shed at the gravel strip and dined on hummus-filled burritos while breathing fumes from spilled aviation fuel.

It finally became obvious that our bush pilot, Paul Klaus wouldn't be arriving to fly us to his wilderness lodge (Ultima Thule) that evening so we dejectedly set up our tents. The grizzled caretaker living in the trailer assured us there hadn't been much bear activity in the area. We still made sure no one had food, toothpaste, soap or any other odorous item in his or her tent.

It rained throughout most of the shortened night and ominous-looking clouds still lingered above us in the morning. Before we could have a breakfast of cold cereal, laser-like shafts of sunlight beamed through the low dark ceiling and the approach of Paul's big Otter bush plane - there were only three of its kind in the world at the time, the other two were in service in Antarctica – could be heard over the flow of the adjacent, glacial-silt laden Chitina River.

We frantically packed up wet tents and uncovered our gear. Paul is notorious for not liking to wait around for passengers to get their act together. After landing, he taxied the aircraft up beside us, swung it around for take-off, revved its powerful engine and then hopped out of the cockpit. He immediately expertly packed the planes fuselage with our gear and supplies. To fit the eleven of us, he had four of us sit in each other's lap on top of duffels and packs stacked between the six small seats located behind the cockpit. We were airborne and breathing more fuel fumes, craning our necks to look out a window, and readying our cameras only fifteen minutes after he landed.

The flight was spectacular. First we flew down the broad lush Chitina Valley where we floated above the Chitina River's braided channels and over numerous lakes and deep side canyons filled with rapids and waterfalls. Then we abruptly banked to the left towards the high Wrangell Mountains and St. Elias Range. As we passed by and over serrated ridges and more-rounded snowcapped peaks, they appeared to be close enough to touch. Finally, we landed on the massive Klutlan glacier at an elevation of approximately 10,500 feet.

Cobalt-blue skies and blistering radiant heat greeted us on the snow-covered glacier. The clear weather allowed the ambient air temperature that night to plummet to 10 degrees below zero.

A snowstorm moved in before morning and the weather continued to deteriorate all day long. Even though its location was identified with a wand, the low-lying clouds and blowing snow made finding the latrine a real challenge. My tent mate and I took turns getting up to shovel snow that kept building up and caving in the sides of our tiny shelter.

On the morning of June 5, a half-dozen Wilson's Warblers blown aloft by the previous night's storm awakened us. They were so disoriented and exhausted that they'd land on our heads when we stood outside our tents. They were all dead within a couple of hours, and the sight of their little yellowish-green bodies littering our campsite brought back the nagging "inner voice" I should've listened to before leaving home.

As new snow continued to accumulate, we heard and sometimes saw avalanches and even an occasional big serac fall on the nearby slopes surrounding us. Finally in the late afternoon the storm began to diminish and visibility improved. The guides used the opportunity to give us a brief lecture on avalanche rescue and to re-acquaint everybody with the use of an avalanche transceiver. We then all took our turn using one of beeping devices to find a transceiver buried in the snow.

That evening the guides packed and distributed group gear and food to carry up the mountain. The plan was to make a carry up to and just over the saddle between Mt. Bona and Mt. Churchill (15,389 feet) to an elevation of about 12,500 to 13,000 feet. Once there we'd leave a cache in the snow and then return to Base Camp. We hoped we'd be able to return to the cache the following day to establish a Camp 1. One or two more, higher camps would then have to be put up before the final push to Mt. Bona's summit.

We buckled on snowshoes, hoisted on our heavy packs, grabbed our ski poles and set off in three rope teams when the visibility finally became passable the next morning. I was second on the lead rope directly behind Sean. Fifty minutes out and almost to the top of a fairly steep but convex-shaped slope he suddenly dropped from sight. I screamed "Falling!" twice as I planted myself in the knee-deep snow. While holding Sean's weight, I was also lying on my spare prussik cords and I was able to move just enough to unclip one of them from my waist harness. I quickly wrapped it around the taut rope leading up to where Sean had disappeared, before realizing that I had no anchor to clip it too. We still had been using ski poles and my ice axe was securely strapped to my pack where I couldn't reach it.

Eric and Cedar were leading the second and third rope teams, respectively. While waiting for them to reach me and provide help, I looked behind me to see how far away they were. I was astonished and just a little upset to see my other two rope team members still standing upright. I yelled for the two of them to kindly please get on the ground.

Eric reached me first and he quickly drove in two pickets. He then gave me another prussik to backup the one I'd previously tied on the rope. After securing the second prussik to the rope, I attached the two of them to the pickets. By that time, Cedar arrived and he began to belay Eric up to the lip of the crevasse so Erik could establish communications with Sean. Cedar then had the second member on his rope team belay him up to Eric. The two assistant guides quickly fashioned together a pulley system and hoisted Sean to the surface.

The crevasse Sean had fallen into was very narrow and it down-sloped to our left. As a consequence after I held his initial fall, he swung downhill and became wedged at a depth of about 20 feet. He was pretty banged up from having bounced off of irregularities in the icy walls. He hurt both of his knees, bruised or possibly fractured his ribs, and had long scrapes on his arms and a severe cut on his left thumb. Before he even stood up, he yelled my name and gave me a bloody thumb up sign for arresting his fall.

We reversed our course and returned to Base Camp. Sean could barely walk, but stubbornly refused to give up his 70-pound pack. Eric, Cedar and I all offered to carry or drag it back but he wouldn't part with it. I worried I'd take a couple of steps too quickly and the rope would pull on him jarring his knees. I continually turned around to ensure that there was a little slack in the rope between us. At the same time I nervously monitored the rope and the two men in front of me. I dreaded that one of them might step on another hidden trapdoor.

When we finally reached the safety of our tents, Eric and Cedar put plastic bags filled with snow on Sean's knees, bandaged his scrapes and cuts, and gave him some meds for pain. When I asked him how he was feeling, he looked me in the eye and said, "Paul, I'm just glad I didn't go any deeper and get wedged any tighter or I'd still be there. Once again, Thanks!"

Excess adrenalin had pooled in my stomach and I felt nauseous. I chewed a couple of Pepto-Bismol, ate some food, and took some more Advil (Vitamin I). Like everybody else I was already routinely taking a couple of the red caplets twice a day for muscle pain.

That night one of the team (a 26 year-old ex-army ranger from Richmond, Illinois) asked to be evacuated. He'd been taking Diamox, but lost his first battle with altitude mountain sickness.

To everyone's surprise, a young Frenchman and two older climbers from Anchorage - down from the summits of both Mts. Bona and Churchill - walked into our camp. They told Sean that Paul was scheduled to fly them out the next morning and that they'd give our sick man a lift back to Anchorage from Chitina.

It snowed all night long and we again woke up to whiteout conditions. It was going to be a rest day anyway to give Sean some time to heal up. When it began to show signs of clearing in the afternoon Sean decided we should make the carry up the mountain.

Unlike Sean, who seemed to have made a miraculous recovery, I had developed sinusitis and my stomach muscles were sore from having held his fall. I also still felt nauseous. After conferring with all three guides, it was agreed that I should stay behind and rest.

I was enviously watching the remainder of the team cautiously picking their way around the previous day's accident site when I heard the distant drone of the Otter. Paul made the traditional low pass over camp before landing. He unloaded part of a large Canadian team and then left without taking on any passengers. I was surprised, but learned that he was coming back with the rest of the Canadians.

Feeling worse and not wanting to become a burden and a safety issue for the team if I went any higher, I decided to leave with the other four. Thanks to my sinusitis, it felt like someone was sticking a sharp stick in my left ear after we lifted off of the glacier and climbed up over the high mountains. The long drive back to Anchorage wasn't anymore comfortable. The ex-ranger and I were crammed into the back two feet of a small pickup's camper stuffed with all of the gear for five climbers. Our knees were almost touching our chins for the entire ride and our backs and behinds felt every rut and pothole.

It was 1 a.m. when we were dropped off in the earthquake prone city. I found a phone, called around desperately looking for a room, and finally got the last one available in the Best Western Barrett Inn.

On the flight home I began to feel pain in my left wrist and side. A visit to Dean Urgent Care in Madison confirmed I'd stressed ligaments in my wrist and bruised or possibly fractured a rib on my left side. I'd fallen on my wrist and ski pole when I arrested Sean's fall. I probably didn't feel any pain at the time because of shock, adrenalin, and of course, I already had Vitamin I in my system.

I learned later that a horrendously complex icefall at about 14,000 feet up Mt. Bona's slopes turned the rest of the team back. They apparently had tried to force a route through it twice and then ran out of time.

My old boss always thought I was crazy for climbing and asked me, "When the heck are you going to buy a fishing license?" Maybe, it's time I did. But more importantly, I need to follow my gut and listen to that "little voice" inside of me.

PENDULUM ON THE PETIT DU CHEVAL

Matt Schonwald was frantically shouting up to me, "Paul! Are you alright?" Still dazed, I felt a moment of nausea pass quickly across me. Then I responded rather meekly -- more to assure myself than him -- "I think so?" Having witnessed my collision with the rock and still very concerned, Schonwald hollered back, "Paul, try and move your arms and legs!" Relief washed over me when I saw and felt each limb obey my thoughts and move.

I finally had made it out to the Cascades in 2003. Two New Yorker's, Chris Catabiano and Jerry "Nikko" Cooke, and I had signed up for what the Seattle-based guiding outfit named Mountain Madness listed as "The Cascade Trilogy". It was an 8-day program that included guided ascents up Mount Adams, Mount Shuksan and Mount Baker.

Nikko, who was tragically killed on Mt. Hood along with two other companions on a winter climb in 2006, had missed his flight connection to Seattle because of a black out in New York City. He didn't arrive in time to join us on the ascent of Mt. Adams, and when he met up with the rest of us in a Seattle restaurant, I assured him over a couple of beers that our climb up the south side of the 11,295-ft. high volcano was a miserable slog with no climbing challenge other than surviving the altitude.

I further told him that the only enjoyable part was being able to do a sitting glissade from the volcano's false summit almost all the way down to the snowline. The glissade had been heavily used and was formed into a chute deep enough in the snow that when you sat down in it you couldn't see over its sides. Descending it was both thrilling and scary at the same time because you gathered speed so quickly it was quite difficult to avoid being ejected from the tube-like slide, especially when you encountered turns.

Over the next five days Matt led the three of us up two of the more outstanding, moderate glacier routes in the North Cascades -- the Sulphide Glacier on Mt. Shuksan and the Easton Glacier on Mt. Baker.

Mount Shuksan is clearly one of the most beautiful and rugged peaks in the North Cascades. The approach to the high, scenic campsites that sit on the west edge of the Sulphide Glacier is quite arduous but rewards you with knockout views of Mount Baker, Shuksan's summit pyramid and the very remote Pickets. The Easton Glacier route on Baker was a straightforward snow and ice climb that only wetted my appetite to do some serious ice climbing.

I met up with Matt again the following year on August 2. A rainy forecast for the entire week for the North Cascades and some washed out roads from large spring storms forced us to change our plans to first climb Forbidden Peak and then the North Face snow and ice route up Mount Logan. Instead Matt drove us to the drier east side of the Cascade Divide where the sun was shining when we checked in at the ranger station in the faux Bavarian Village of Leavenworth. A ranger informed us that there was a big fire burning near where we wanted to hike into the rugged 576,900 acre Glacier Peak Wilderness. But the area to the west of Phelps Creek wasn't closed and we drove north from Leavenworth to Chiwawa River Road. The narrow paved road eventually turns to gravel and finally just muddy ruts long before it ends at the 3,600-foot high Phelps Creek Trailhead.

The first six miles of hiking that Monday afternoon is a pleasant walk. The trail is part of the famous Pacific Coast Trail and it only gains 600 feet in elevation over that distance. The real backbreaking labor began when we headed up a mile and a half long side trail that skirts the north branch of Leroy Creek. The path leads almost straight up for 2,800 feet.

It turned out to be a very hot and humid day. Our T-shirts beneath the load of our packs stuck to our backs and the smell of sunscreen and our sweat commingled with the sticky smell of pine needles, resin, and the dry, windblown earth.

Grasshoppers were everywhere and sounded like rattlesnakes when they took flight in front of us. Then Black fly's and mosquito's greeted us where we stopped to camp in a small meadow located at approximately 7,000 feet and just below the 9,100-foot high peak named Seven-Fingered Jack. We ate a quick dinner and dove inside our clammy tent to foil the pesky bugs.

Matt set his alarm for 4 a.m., but rain patter on our tent's fly woke us up around 3:00. The precipitation increased but when it began to subside at 5:30, Matt fetched the stove and fired it up in the tent's vestibule. By the time we'd swallowed a lukewarm cup of watery instant oatmeal and washed it down with a swig of weak coffee the overcast sky began to clear.

Matt's plan was for us to climb a normally snow-filled gully that leads directly up Mt. Maude's North Face to its 9,060-foot high summit. First we had to ascend three high passes, descend most of the Entiat Glacier, and then traverse the Entiat Icefall to get over to the gully. Then after climbing up to Maude's summit we'd have to descend her two-mile long South Ridge back down to the second high pass and from there retrace almost half of our approach route to get back to our camp.

It was 6:00 a.m. when we grabbed our packs and headed south toward fields of talus scattered below Mt. Maude's East Face.

The only diversion while hiking the six miles to the Entiat Glacier was stealing a quick look at the flat-topped wall of cloud flowing – like a vaporized waterfall – over and down the huge pass separating Fortress Mountain and Buck Mountain located seven miles to the west of us, and when we crested the second pass to see the stunning view of Ice Lakes cradled in two large cirques below Mt. Maude's South Face. After descending the second pass we hiked for another two hours on talus covered ledges 300 feet above the two lakes.

We reached the top of the third pass at 11:00 a.m. We then put on crampons, roped up, and began the descent of the Entiat Glacier. Below a ridge of rock between the upper glacier and the Entiat Icefall we saw the snow in the gully we came to climb was discontinuous in four places. We were left with two options: Retreat back to camp the way we'd come or explore a route up the Entiat Icefall. Long steep falls are best avoided. But neither one of us wanted to climb back up the glacier and face the six miles of foot-bruising talus again so we decided to see if it'd go.

Our first problem was finding a way to get across a deep slot that had been cut by melt water rushing down between the lower glacier and

Cloud waterfall flowing down between Fortress Mountain
and Buck Mountain. (Photo by author)

the icefall. The width and depth of the natural barrier increased further down slope. We chose to climb 100 feet back up the glacier's 30-degree slope of dirty snow. Then we traversed an icy section that had rivulets of melt water flowing on top of it to where we could carefully descend the glacier's steep eastern edge down to a small shelf of ice that extended out over a big gap.

Once we were finally on the icefall we simul-climbed close together for several hundred feet over and around numerous, convoluted crevasses. We aimed for where the ice flowed around the end of an exposed black rock bench that runs diagonally across a portion of the North Face. The ice had obviously flowed over the bench in the past since a wall of contorted seracs (house-sized towers and pinnacles of ice), exists directly below it.

It was nearing the heat of the day and we could only hope the seracs weren't in a state of near or total collapse as we passed below them. The ice towers emitted spooky pops and groans and lower down along the

Author peering back down drop to Ice lakes.
(Photo by Matt Schonwald)

fall's terminus huge blocks boomed like reverberating thunder as they tumbled down towards the deep glacial valley bounded by Mt. Maude, Seven-Fingered Jack and Mt. Fernow.

At one point Matt had to scale a small pressure ridge. He slipped near its top and slid down the other side of the buckled ice onto a fragile layer of snow and ice bridging over a crevasse. Under his weight it shifted loudly, sank a foot, and then tilted towards the melt water washing debris down along the fall's east margin. I held my breath. He'd come perilously close to being dumped into the crevasse or even worst the cascading water that further down flowed beneath the ice.

The higher we went the sportier and more difficult the climbing became. We encountered sections as steep as 80 degrees and had to take turns using the two technical ice tools we had between us to overcome the shorter vertical to overhanging walls on the upper end of multiple bergschrunds -- large crevasses filled with sunken bridges of snow and ice. Matt also had only brought three ice screws. We could've used four to provide for proper belays and at least one more to provide some protection between them. We each carried a picket (aluminum stake) for protection in the snow gully but they were useless on the icefall.

About 1,000 feet above our starting point we faced a second wall of seracs just below the fall's final headwall. This time the seracs extended across the entire width of the fall. We both sensed the exposure growing beneath us and wondered out loud how hard it'd be to safeguard a descent back down to the glacier if we'd reached an impasse.

As we neared the threatening wall we spotted a large melt-out cavity in the serac leaning against the rock ridge confining the eastern edge of the ice. Instead of climbing up into it though we first tried to go up and over the serac by scaling the rock. Matt gained about 15 feet and placed a tricam. There were few if any cracks in the rock above him to place additional protection and he wisely decided to

Author at belay stance on Icefall. (Photo by Matt Schonwald)

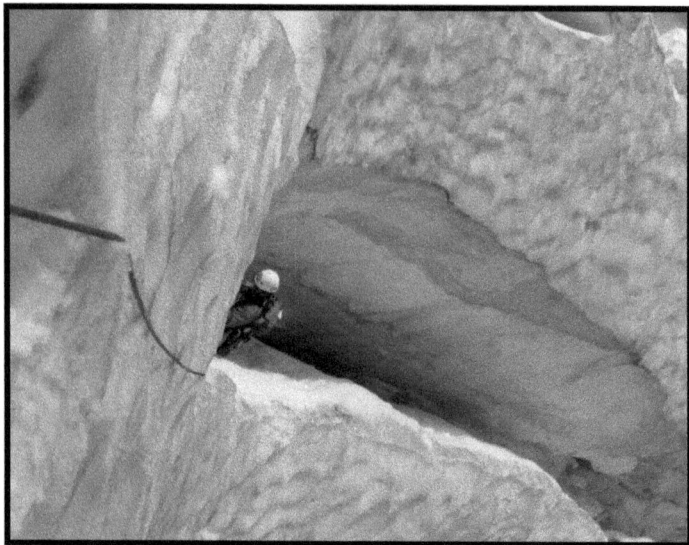

Author ascending vertical section of Icefall.
(Photo by Matt Schonwald)

lower off of the tricam down into the ice-roofed cavern. I joined him and after retrieving the rope and leaving behind the tricam we spelunked to the other side of the serac. A foot-wide ledge fortunately ran along its back wall just above a sizeable open crevasse. The narrow ledge, however, dead-ended at a short vertical step. Fortunately a narrow arch provided access from the top of the step up to the headwall.

Two full rope pitches (almost 400 ft.) of front pointing took us up the short step, the ladder-like arch and the 70-degree headwall. Another 200 feet of walking over low-angle snow enabled us to finally step off of the ice onto a small pass up on Maude's West Ridge. It was 4 p.m.

The two-hour rain delay in the morning had caught up to us. The weather began to look iffy and it was still a long way up easy to moderately hard rock along the ridge to the actual summit.

We ate our lunch, reluctantly decided our climb was over, and began descending the south side of the mountain. Eventually we encountered a 100-foot rappel and that enabled us to scramble down to a snowfield that provided an easy path to the ledges above Ice Lakes. Ironically, we still ended up having to hike back over two of the high passes and almost all of talus-covered approach route we ascended that morning. We arrived back at our tent at 8:30 p.m.

The next morning while descending to the car blisters on my ankles broke and reformed before we reached the more level Phelps Creek Trail. I remember muttering to myself whether I was having fun yet. But after grabbing a beer, burger and fries in Leavenworth all of the pain and suffering was forgotten.

That afternoon we drove back to Matt's house in Seattle to pick up some extra rock climbing gear. We then drove north before heading back east on the Famous Cascade Highway (Hwy. 20). Thunder, lightening and water vapor rising off of the hot, wet pavement greeted us up on Rainy Pass. The misty vapors swirling in the beam of our headlights was hypnotic. "I think we've just entered the Twilight Zone," Matt quipped. The actual storm was just ahead of us, but stars were out when we drove into the Early Winter's Campground located just up the road from Mazama at 10:30 p.m.

We had wanted to climb the Classic Becky Route on Liberty Bell and the Cave Route on Concord Tower on Thursday. Then maybe the more challenging Kangaroo Ridge on Friday. All three are fairly long and moderately difficult Alpine rock climbs located near Washington Pass.

But it poured on Thursday morning, and we ended up joining local climbers getting their caffeine and sugar fix in the Mazama Bakery. The forecast for Friday was for even heavier showers. Everybody there was astounded by the weather. It's not supposed to rain, yet alone pour, in Mazama during the summer.

After lunch at the Winthrop Brew Pub, the precipitation stopped just long enough for us to top-rope four climbs at a crag called Fun Rock. The 80-120 foot high black wall of limestone is just a mile up the road from Mazama. When it started raining again we drove the eastern end of the Washington Cascade Loop back to Leavenworth. The sky was totally clear that night at the Swiftwater Campground located just off of Hwy. 2.

In the morning we climbed halfway up a hard six-pitch (500 foot) route on Castle Rock in Icicle Canyon. It started to sprinkle and we reached the car just before it began to pour. And it continued to rain after a soggy lunch beneath the park shelter downtown.

We drove back to Winthrop and had fish and chips for dinner at the brewpub. Are you starting to see a pattern here? Needless to say my food and mileage costs were exceeding my budget for the trip.

Actually we returned to Mazama because one of the owners of the North Cascades Guide School had given us a hand drawn topo and some beta for a new climb called Spontaneity Ridge. The arête-like ridge is located on the right hand side of the Petit du Cheval. The approach to the climb is fairly obvious. A rock Cairn below the big pullover at mile marker 165 on Highway 20 indicates where you descend directly down the road's steep rocky embankment. At the bottom of the embankment a path marked with surveyor's tape leads into the heavy-forested valley. Eventually you have to cross a large log over a stream. Then the faint trail peters out at the base of a steep, brushy talus and scree-covered slope several hundred feet below the start of the climb. More Cairns, surveyor's tape and some brush cuttings indicate the best way to attack the slope. There is also a fixed rope protecting a very exposed traverse.

The actual climb involves two (100 foot) moderately hard pitches, a long section of low angle scrambling protected by another fixed rope on an exposed part of the section, and finally five (50-100 foot) somewhat harder pitches. The quality of the rock on the two lower pitches was disappointing. It consists of rotten, orange granite covered with very slippery, black lichen and a lot of unattached blocks. The upper five pitches though are quite worthwhile. They consist of solid, clean white granite with some nice finger and hand cracks.

We topped out on the pinnacle-like summit at 3:30 p.m. The descent down to the low angle section of the climb involves three rappels. The last one is dead vertical and isn't in line with the next anchor. Matt went first and ended up having to climb back up to where he could traverse across a low angle, cliffy slope to reach the offset anchor. After clipping into a nylon sling slung around a stout tree, he cautioned me several times to keep to the right.

I could hear him, but couldn't see him. I started traversing to the right as directed and encountered a broad steep ramp. It was a real struggle to stay on the sloping rock because the rope was now taut and trying to pull me back off to my left. I launched myself toward a nice finger crack just out of my reach, just as I was about to grasp it the rope and gravity won the tug of war and pulled me off. I then swung like a weighted pendulum for 40 feet before slamming butt first into a left facing dihedral of smooth yellow granite.

I remember hearing a sickening smack and feeling the jarring collision. Then almost simultaneously, my helmet collided with the unforgiving rock wall and I momentarily lost consciousness.

When I began to regain my senses it took me a moment to comprehend where I was and what I was doing dangling over a thousand feet above the Cascade Highway. I remember focusing enough to inspect the back-up prussik I had wrapped around the rappel rope and clipped the remaining loop to my leg harness to keep me from sliding off the end of the rope if for any reason my brake hand should come off of the rope.

The route named Spontaneity Ridge goes up the right edge
of the Petit du Cheval. (Photo by author)

Author beginning a rappel in the South Dakota Needles.
(Photo by Lenore Sobota)

About the same time I looked down and everything below me appeared totally out of focus, and that really put a scare in me until I felt for my glasses and found that the force of my impact had knocked them off. I cussed myself out for having left my older pair and my Croakies in the car.

When I spit out another mouth full of blood my foggy brain registered that my tongue was still numb, and I muttered to myself, "Dang, did I bite right through it?" I lost my nerve to touch it to find out.

View from the summit of the Petit du Cheval shows the Cascade Highway below and the Liberty Bell Formation in the distance. (Photo by author)

Matt yelled out for me to shake my limbs to establish if they were all working properly. All four fortunately moved as directed by my thoughts. Then I slowly lowered myself down to where I could very carefully traverse up to Matt's stance.

After immediately clipping me into his anchor, he checked out my back and questioned me whether I felt any tingling or numbness in my fingers or toes. Nothing seemed to be out of place in my spinal chord and my digits were all working properly.

My tongue was still numb and I asked Matt to look at it. "It looks like you bit it in at least four places," he said. The injury wasn't as severe as I'd feared and thanks to evolution, the bleeding had already stopped. I really didn't realize I was indeed hurt until I could feel my rear end pulsing whenever I stopped moving, but the pain was bearable.

Matt belayed me down the first fixed rope. Then instead of trying to scramble down the rest of the low angle section of rock and having to do two more rappels down the two lower rock pitches we un-roped and cut over to a nearby scree chute.

Matt stayed close and in front of me in case I took a tumble. Following the edge of the scree chute downward was nerve-racking, slow, and quite painful. Normally, we'd have taken the scree chute in bounds and rocks would scatter in front of us, clatter off of each other and follow us down.

I had trouble seeing where to step without my glasses, and every footfall jolt to my frame brought considerable pain from my tailbone area. When I passed some gas I grinned and tried to make light of our situation by telling Matt, "Well, at least that still works and you're not right behind me." He laughed, albeit uneasily.

At the base of the climb we retrieved our stashed packs, put on our hiking boots, and Matt again belayed me as I crossed the traverse on the lower fixed rope.

We finally reached Matt's car at 7:30. I swallowed some Advil and then hung onto the grab bar on the ceiling of the little Honda Civic and pulled myself up enough to elevate my rear whenever we went over a bump. We were both starving so we stopped in Marblemount to eat at a small drive-in. I had my first shower in six days when our waitress accidentally dumped Matt's 20-ounce Coke on me. It clearly wasn't my day or night.

From Marblemount we drove to the hospital in Sedro-Woolley. We arrived at the emergency room at 10:00 p.m., and waited two hours before I got my pelvis X-rayed. It's a good thing they didn't have me lay on my coke-covered stomach I probably would've stuck to the leather table. Then dressed in a hospital gown I waited another two hours in a cold room on a cold examining table before I got to see a doctor, who informed me that I'd fractured my sacral bone. A half hour later an apologetic nurse poked me in the rear with a stinging shot of morphine and another shot with something to help prevent nausea.

It was 5 a.m. when I finally hit the sack at a Holiday Inn near SEA-TAC. I slept until 4:30 p.m. that Sunday. I tried to fly home that day, but they couldn't get me from Minneapolis to Madison. I had to return to the hotel for another night. Then when I flew home on Monday I got a tour beneath the Seattle and Minneapolis Terminals in a wheelchair. I remember handing the porter that had wheeled me to my gate at Sea-Tac $5. He looked me in the eye and said, "That's not enough sir."

Looking back on this adventure my helmet saved my life, and if I'd hit the wall feet first I probably would've broken my ankles or one or both of my legs. I then would've had a "Touching the Void" experience of having to crawl down to the car or, even worse, I would've had to be rescued. My glasses cost $340. As for my tongue it gave me an excuse to eat lots of ice cream.

When my brother-in-law, who lives in Colorado, heard the news he sent me a quote from a friend that he said looks at life like I do. "My Life is not a journey to the grave with the intention of arriving safely in a pretty and well preserved body, but rather to skid in broadside, thoroughly used up, totally worn out and loudly proclaiming-WOW, what a ride!" I agree and I was back climbing as soon as I healed up. But in hindsight I always knew this was the accident and subsequent injury that was going to limit my mobility in the future.

A NASTY SLIP

There's a saying climbers have, "There's a lot of bold climbers but there's no old, bold climbers." You'd think I'd know my limitations by the age of 60.

While trying to bridge between two of the huge, stone columns of Devil's Tower lactic acid was burning in my arms, my legs were also shaking from accumulated strain. I shifted most of my weight to my two left limbs.   Then at the precise moment I removed my right hand to shake it and my swelled forearm to get the blood moving my left foot shot off the tiny edge where I had it smeared on the side of the other octagonal column.

Lenore Sobota and Anne Meyer, two members of the Rushmore Gang, had picked me up on September 22. Another member of the gang, Anne's dad Dave, caught up with us three days later at our campsite in the Black Hills.

On this trip, besides climbing in the spectacular pinnacles of the South Dakota Needles, we again took the side trip to northeastern Wyoming to climb Devil's Tower.

Our favorite campground in the Black Hills is located near two of the areas where we climbed -- just behind Mount Rushmore National Monument and below the dam holding back Custer State Park's picturesque Sylvan Lake. After erecting our tents, we warmed up on a few of the short, easy climbs at the Rushmore area.

The next day, we did several longer routes in the same area. The last climb I led that afternoon is called Shark's Breath. It's a stunning route, where 11 fixed bolts lead up to an anchor bolt system placed just below the 100-foot high granite formation's 1-foot wide rim. The actual formation is aptly named Shark Fin. I've never climbed it before so I had no idea how many bolts there were to clip. And at the time, I only had eight draws (short, nylon slings with a carabiner attached to each end) hooked on my waist harness and ended up having to skip three of the last four bolts on the hardest part of the route to get to the belay anchor. Climbers clip one end of a draw to a bolt and the other end to their rope so if they fall, they'll only drop twice the distance they're above the last clipped bolt. Obviously, for me falling on Shark's Breath wasn't an option.

The following day, a wind advisory was issued for the entire Black Hills region. While leading one of the higher climbs at Sylvan Lake, I had to stop and hang on a number of times. And after belaying Anne up to the top of it, a 45-mph gust blew my hat off. It landed on a shelf of rock behind the climb. After rappelling down the climb, I scrambled almost 100 feet up the easier backside of the rock formation to retrieve the cap. I was hoping the whole time that the next day's issue of the Rapid City Journal wouldn't contain the line -- "Foolish 60 year-old dies from fall at Sylvan Lake, while trying to fetch old hat."

The next day, we wanted to repeat the standard route on Spire Four the four of us did in 2004. Unfortunately, high winds from the day before ushered in a cold front and it rained on and off until 3 p.m.

Instead, we enjoyed a leisurely breakfast at Mount Rushmore. We then drove the wildlife loop in Custer State Park, before climbing some short routes in the Rushmore area from 4:00 until dark. The others just wanted to hike. But I insisted we take our climbing gear just in case. When we returned to Lenore's SUV, the temperature was 42 degrees. It dropped to 29 degrees that evening.

We woke up to a crisp, clear morning with a hard frost on our tents. After repeating some of the climbs at the Rushmore area, we packed up and drove to Devil's Tower. The fall colors along Highway 385 from Hill City to Deadwood were spectacular. We were also treated to one of the most gorgeous sunsets we've ever seen as we traveled along Highway 14, just west and north of Sturgis, WY.

Andy Petefish, owner of Tower Guides and our friend, had invited us to camp on his six-acre property, which is located just south of Devil's Tower off of Hwy. 14.

That night I was awakened by what sounded like large, hoofed animals running around near my tent. There had been a number of mule deer on Andy's property when we returned from dinner. But then I heard dogs barking from the ranch house down the road and deer snort and run away. Lying with my ear to the ground I heard a soft padding that was just audible approaching toward my tent. My heart began pounding as the animal crept right up to my tent. The night sky was totally clear with a bright, almost full moon nearly overhead illuminating the outside of my tent. Suddenly, the shadow of a rather large, round face with whiskers and pointed ears appeared on the tent sidewall right in front of my face. Like the title of Barry Alvarez's autobiography, "Don't Flinch," I didn't, and neither did it. Finally, I broke the impasse and hit the tent fabric with my fist. Whatever it was -- I'm convinced it was a mountain lion -- ran away. I held my breath afraid to make a sound for several seconds. When my heart ceased pounding, I found the courage to sit up, unzip the screen door and peer outside. Seeing nothing, I lay back down scared to fall back asleep. I eventually dozed off just before dawn.

When everybody collected around Andy's picnic table for breakfast, I mentioned my nighttime visitor. They all laughed. "It must have been the neighbor's horses," Lenore said. She then pointed out the two white mares standing out in the large pasture adjacent to Andy's property. I hadn't seen the horses when we arrived just before darkness the night before. My tent was 100 feet or so from everybody else's, and within 10 feet of the strands of barbwire that enclosed the pasture. I think it may have been the horses nervously sauntering around that initially woke me up. They smelled the mountain lion, then snorted and ran away when the big cat approached too close.

After a few more laughs at my expense, and a quick, cold breakfast, we left to climb Devil's Tower. Over the years, I've made the difficult ascent nine times by six different routes. And I wanted to repeat a route I climbed in 1989. Unlike most climbing areas, the Tower's routes are quite sustained. The weight of a second rope needed for rappelling, all of the extra gear necessary to protect a route, and the water you have to carry adds to the difficulty of climbing there.

Anne and I began climbing around 10:00. The first, and so-called warm up pitch is 160 feet long. It begins just above the massive boulder field of fallen and broken columns that lie at the Tower's base. It's also located right below an area notorious for rock fall, called the "Bowling Alley." In other words, it's not a place you want to hang around.

The second pitch cuts across and angles up a short, awkward 40-foot section to a large ledge. Behind the ledge is a box-like area enclosed by two very large and tall columns. Between the two columns is a gap where another column once stood. The pitch continues up the right side of the left column for another 80 feet to fixed anchors placed just above the top of the column.

While angling across and up the awkward start of the second pitch, I reached above my head to place a piece of protection into a narrow finger-size crack. But to my surprise the crack was filled with wasps. I pulled my hand back very slowly, and then continued on without protection. The little, winged devil's fortunately ignored me. After hoisting myself up onto the large ledge and entering the alcove, I hesitated. The rest of the pitch looked a lot harder and more difficult to protect than the route I remembered having climbed 17 years ago.

Lenore and Dave had hired Andy to take them up the Durrance, which is the easiest, and therefore most popular route on the Tower. At the time they were already well above me. Believing I had to be off-route, I yelled up to Andy for directions. Seeing where I was, he shouted back down, "Paul! Bridge up the left side."

I struggled up about 15 feet, decided to reverse directions, and climbed back down to Anne to discuss alternatives. I couldn't stomach just retreating. Besides I knew Anne really wanted to join her dad on the summit. We both agreed that our best option was to just down climb to where we could traverse over to the base of the Durrance. I've led the Durrance four times before, including finishing the climb by going up what's called the Bailey Direct twice.

But then, "Paul!" Andy yelled. "Do you want me to throw you a rope? You can then swing over to the Durrance or climb up to the next anchor on top of the column. Your choice."

Because of pride and indecision, I reluctantly accepted Andy's offer of help. It took him two tosses. Anne caught the end of the rope the second time. I made another bad decision after tying it to my harness and continued back up the hard pitch. It seemed like a good idea at the time, because Anne had heard another party of climbers arrive at the base of the Durrance.

I quickly passed by the wasps for the third time. "They're waiting for you," I jokingly told Anne. "Oh, thanks!" she replied.

After stemming up about 20 feet this time, my left foot flew off of the edge of the column just as I had shifted my weight to it. I only fell a short distance, because Andy had me on a top belay. But my left thumb was bent backwards on the rock column with the full force of my falling body.

Andy and Anne hearing me cry out in pain inquired almost simultaneously, "Paul! Are you okay?" The thumb began to swell

173

immediately. I grimaced and responded, "I think I broke my thumb." Then with Andy's encouragement and patience I continued up to the anchors.

Stemming with two hands was difficult. It was a nightmare with only one good hand. I almost fell every time I inadvertently banged the injured thumb on the crystallized rock. And my right shoulder and bicep muscle were so strained by the ascent that they were still sore several months later.

When I reached the top of the column and clipped into the anchor bolts, Andy had Lenore put me on belay. He then climbed the next higher pitch on the Durrance and belayed Dave up it.

When I caught my breath, I belayed Anne up to me. After she joined me, we had to traverse over to the start of another pitch on a different route next to the Durrance. I was totally demoralized when I reached the base of it and looked up to see that I'd have to stem up another 120 feet, before a short traverse would take me over to where Lenore was perched.

Not satisfied with almost breaking my thumb, shortly after starting up the pitch I slipped and bent it back a second time. No doubt the tourists on the trail that winds around the base of the Tower heard me howl this time, as much in frustration as from the pain.

My rack (gear that a lead climber places for protection) hanging from a sling looped over my left shoulder became my nemesis. Instead of providing me with protection, it routinely got stuck between the rock column and my waist. I spent loads of energy every time I had to grab it, lift it, and then fling it behind my back -- only to have it swing right back.

I began to hyperventilate and hung on the rope at least twice to try to slow my breathing. But I just couldn't do it. Where's a paper bag when you need one?

I knew better but I kept looking up anyway. Every time I did, it seemed like I had further to go. I eventually just wanted to give up. But what was I going to do? I couldn't just hang there. And nobody was going to haul me up. Once again, with the help of my fellow climbers, I had to get myself out of a tough situation. No rescue was coming, nor did I want one.

When I finally reached Lenore's belay stance, I almost passed out. I probably just stood up too fast, or maybe it had something to do with the combinations of not breathing properly, pain, stress, dehydration, and a poor night's sleep. Whatever, it scared Lenore and me both since we were 300 feet above the boulder field.

I couldn't catch my breath, and Lenore had to remind me to take some deep breaths to force some oxygen into my lungs. Then I managed to drink a small bottle of Gatorade. It revived me just enough to belay Anne up, while Lenore climbed the next pitch to where Andy had left Dave clipped in.

In the meantime, Andy had climbed up above a short, but very exposed move called the "Jump Traverse," to one of the main rappel anchors for descending the Tower. He then threaded his rope through its eyebolts and rappelled down to the large, grassy ledge called the "Meadows."

After Anne and I climbed up to join Lenore and Dave, Andy belayed us one at a time as we swung across the abyss -- a vertical drop of 350 feet -- to where we could climb up to him.

On the summit, I found myself questioning my judgment. Anne and I should have just retreated, especially after we heard the other climbing party at the base of the Durrance. But I figured with Andy's belay once I got up to the next anchor, I could lead the next higher two pitches of the harder route to the Meadows. And, of course, Anne would've been very disappointed if we had gone down. It was her dad's 29th trip up the Tower, and at age 78 it was his last, and I thought probably even his last climb.

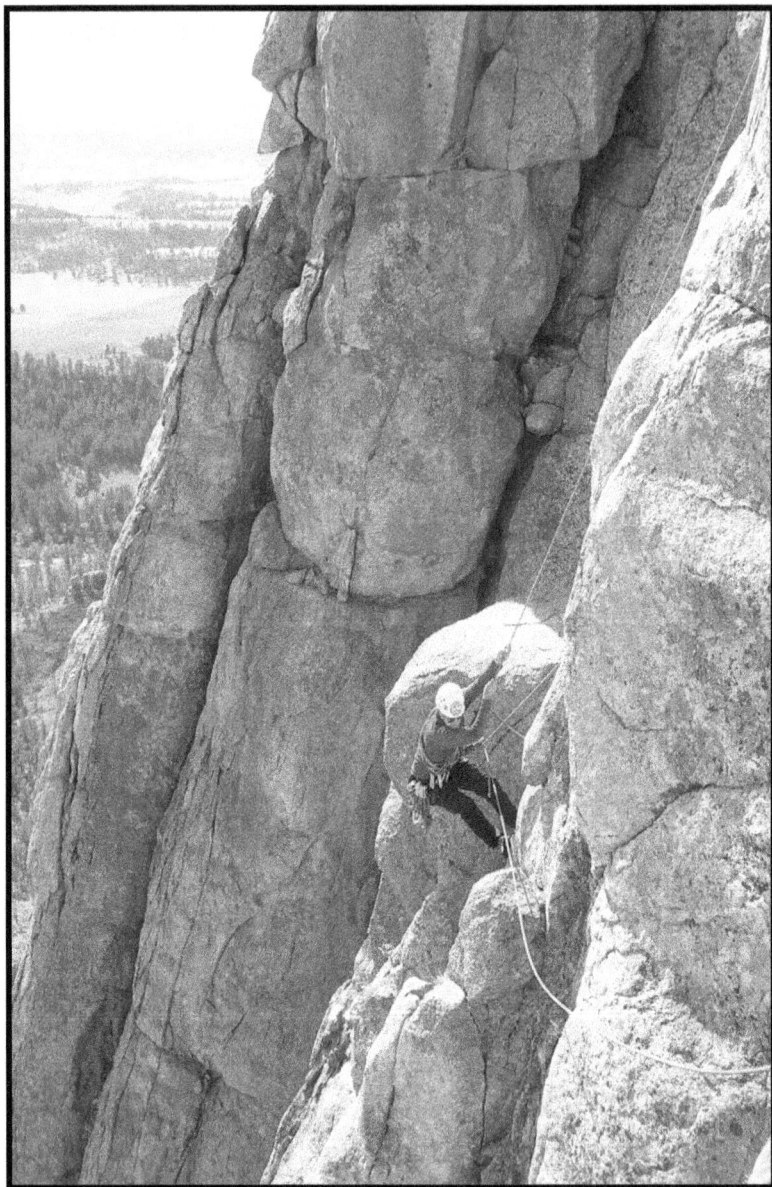

Author swinging across gap to reach short pitch up to the "Meadows" on Devil's Tower. (Photo by Lenore Sobota)

The Rushmore Gang (from the left: the author, Lenore Sobota, Anne and Dave Meyer) on Devil's Tower summit with friend Andy Petefish. (Photo by author)

It was the third time I was injured during my last four climbing trips. On the long drive home, I again found myself pondering if I should hang up my rope. Most climbers a lot younger than me quit the sport due to career and/or family pressures. But then there's a very select few climbers like Dave Meyer.

After getting back home I heard that I was just another baby boomer not ready to act my age. But I still felt the need to gain some elevation every year and continued to climb. I did however finally take up another safer outdoor activity. I bought a bike, and biking quickly became my second outdoor passion.

ROLE MODEL

D ave Meyer is an unusual man and my role model. He's inspired me with his enthusiasm for exercise ever since I first met him in 1989, while I was helping to lead a group of Iowa Mountaineers on climbs of Devil's Tower. Dave, a tall lean and bearded pharmacist had just retired from the Upjohn Company in his hometown of Kalamazoo, Michigan after putting in 33 years. Other jobs I'm aware of that he's held include farmhand, helping to build the Alaska Highway during World War II, and working as a gold miner after the so-called highway was completed. But Dave's most unusual job came while still a student at Iowa University, when he was hired to replace the man who changed the big light bulbs at the top of the five radio towers located around Iowa City, Iowa.

After the Iowa Mountaineers Devil's Tower Outing, we've climbed together on and off since 1995. We've not only spent a lot of time together in the Black Hills Needles and Cathedral Spires, but we've enjoyed each others company on a couple of longer road trips to Rocky Mountain National Park and to other popular climbing crags located in Colorado and southern Wyoming.

Dave made his 29th ascent of Devil's Tower in 2006. On that trip I had turned 60 and three days later he celebrated his 78th birthday. Before arriving at the Tower this time, I once again led him and his daughter Anne and Lenore Sobota up several climbs in the Needles located just behind and below Mount Rushmore National Monument and near Sylvan Lake in South Dakota's Custer State Park.

The climb named Creeping Senility is located on one of the higher granite formations near Sylvan Lake. The formation is appropriately called Old People's Dome. In 1994, Dave and I made a pact at the top of the climb that we would climb it together when he turned 80 and when I began drawing Social Security at age 62.

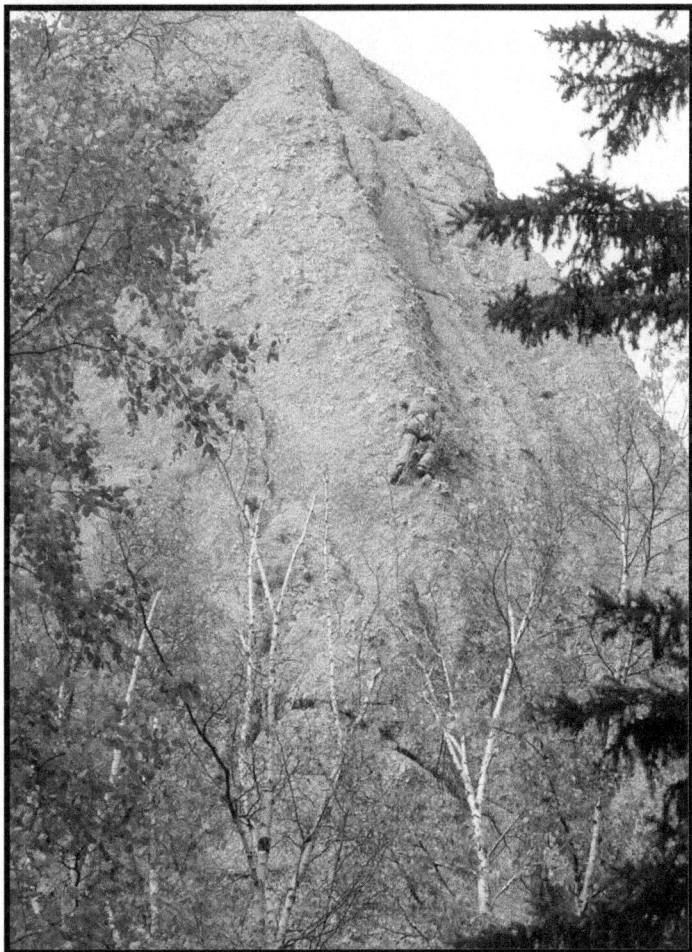

Author leading Creeping Senility. (Photo by Lenore Sobota)

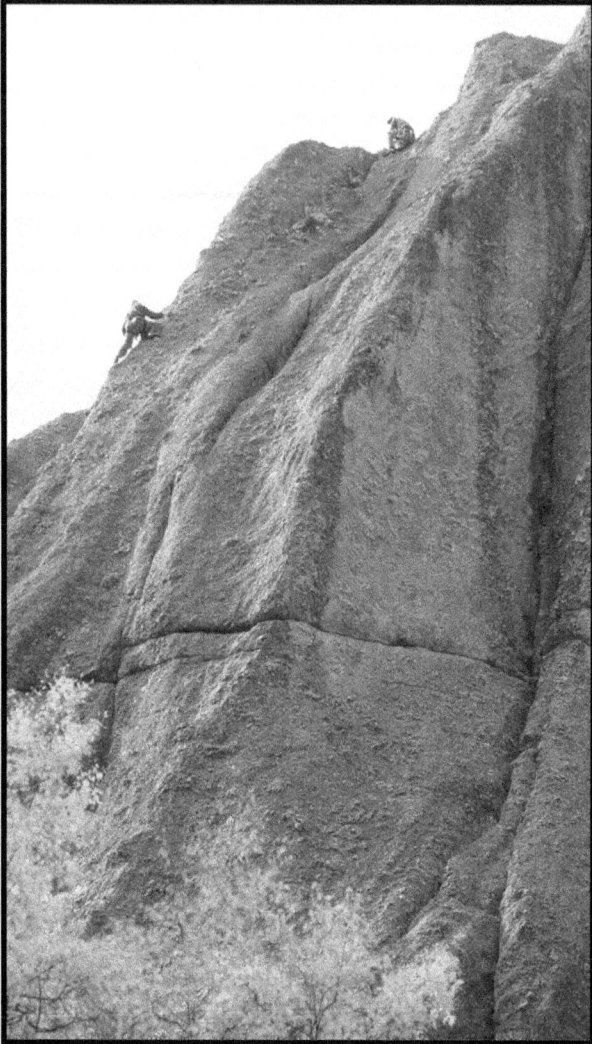

Author belaying Anne Meyer up Creeping Senility.
(Photo by Lenore Sobota)

Dave has also run and skied for 40 years. A wall in his den is covered with medals and ribbons from competing in countless races, and he spent several weeks each winter downhill skiing in Colorado and Michigan's Upper Peninsula. Skiing actually has been his most dangerous activity according to an article written about him in "Generations," a Michigan newspaper magazine. That's because he's broken his ribs three times while skiing after becoming airborne each time and landing on his chest. Dave even has tried his hand at snowboarding. The same magazine story states a classic Dave quip, "My expert moves with a snowboard are to fall down and sit in the snow."

Dave Meyer ascending Creeping Senility.
(Photo by Lenore Sobota)

Unfortunately, Dave may not be able to run or ski anymore. But his limitations have more to do with battling cancer than his age. David's treatments derailed our plans to do the Creeping Senility climb together that fall when he turned 80. His legendary stamina is now significantly diminished, yet he refused to not try to do the climb the following summer and we achieved our goal that July.

Dave even managed to ascend two other climbs, including a new, unnamed route we found the day before heading back to Devil's Tower.

When we arrived at the Devil's Tower Visitor Center it was 94 degrees in the shade. I had little energy due to a lack of sleep, while camping the previous week and my hands were sore and swollen from climbing several routes on the extremely coarse rock in the Needles. I also had used a lot of nervous energy, while doing a couple of dead-end, but hard exploratory ascents in the Cathedral Spires.

I had trouble later in the day communicating and even recognizing where I was when eating pizza in the small, isolated, cowboy town of Hulett, Wyoming.

The plan had been for all of us to camp on a friend's property out in the boonies, but the rest of the gang convinced me that what I most needed was a really good night's sleep in a motel room. After checking the three motels in town I settled on staying in a little A-frame cabin where I took a very, very long, hot shower and then slept from 8:30 p.m. to 8:10 a.m. I would have probably slept right through the checkout time of 10:00, and missed one of the best breakfasts in the West at the Ponderosa Bar and Café if the cleaning lady hadn't knocked on my door. She didn't realize that I was still there since there was no car parked outside.

There was to be no climb of Devil's Tower for Dave or me on the trip. We just joined the tourist's on the trail winding around the talus at the base of the unique monolith, while Anne and Lenore made an attempt with local Guide and friend, Andy Petefish.

I again found myself wondering if the trip was my last opportunity to climb with Dave. I knew at the time if it was, I was really going to miss his whaler's beard smile, ever present positive attitude, and the tall tales about his unique life experiences, even though I've heard him tell them many times.

I feel privileged to have spent time with Dave Meyer. He's taught me to never let age keep you down and that older people can do so much more than most people believe. We just have to keep moving, be excited about living and be willing to try. Unfortunately, Dave never climbed with us again.

THE BAD, THE GOOD, AND THE ALMOST UGLY

T HE BAD: My latest and hopefully my last climbing injury occurred
on April 19, 2010. It was a beautiful Sunday morning and I was
climbing at Devil's Lake State Park with David Heitke. I had met
David the previous summer at a campground in the Black Hills. My legs
were exceptionally sore from having climbed with him the day before
and from nearly running with the load of a heavy pack down the 1,400
stone steps of the Potholes Trail. In a hurry to get home for dinner, I also
skipped stretching out my calves and thighs when I reached my car.

The next morning, I found myself struggling to lead the first climb we
attempted. It's a moderate climb on the West bluff named "The Bone,"
and I've led it several times before over the years. This time my legs
were so weak and sore I barely completed the climb without falling. It
was a subtle warning of what was to come that I failed to heed.

After belaying David up it I constructed an anchor on the top of an
adjacent climb called "Jacob's Ladder". It's another moderate climb that
I've led a few times in the past.

David studied the route as he rappelled down it and decided he
wanted to lead it. Like many of the climbs at Devil's Lake its crux, which
involves surmounting a small roof-like feature, favors taller climbers.
And, unlike myself, David has the necessary reach and made the
awkward moves look easy. But being shorter than him, I have to stand
on a ledge below the roof on my tiptoes to reach the handholds above it.
Then I have do a pull up and at the same time raise my right foot above
my waist in order to place my big toe on the slanting lip of the roof. I
then have to stand up on the tenuous toehold to reach a higher and more
secure left hand jam, before I can crab my left leg up the underlying,
virtually-smooth rock face beneath the roof in order to securely place
both feet on top of the roof.

When I attempted to straighten out my right leg this time to stand
up on the toehold I was jolted by a powerful pull behind my knee
followed by a sharp pain in my calf muscle.

Belaying me from above David heard me cry out and queried, "Paul, are you all right?"

I responded between gasps from the pain, "My leg just went out!" Hanging by my hands my arms quickly tired and I yelled, "Falling!" David had already tightened the belay and easily arrested my fall. Hanging by my harness I instinctively reached back up and grabbed the poor handholds above the roof to pull myself back on the rock. But then instructed David, "Just lower me; there's no way I can continue to climb."

When I landed at the base of the climb on my good leg for support I quickly untied from the rope and hopped over to a nearby flat rock, collapsed, and watched my calf swell up to almost as big as my thigh.

Depression immediately began to build as I thought about having to cancel two upcoming trips and losing my hard won fitness. Staying fit at my age is becoming more difficult every year. Like my friend, Bill Fisher, always tells me when I complain about my aches and pains, "Paul you're not a young man anymore."

David rappelled down and quickly produced a cell phone from his pack. "Do you want me to call 911?" he asked.

Being a strong advocate of personal responsibility in the acceptance of risk and, like most of the climbers I know, believing that calling for a rescue is a huge failure, I emphatically said, "No way!"

I feared the descent ahead of me but I was determined to get down under my own steam – even if it meant sliding the whole way there on my butt. Having survived other injuries in actual wilderness settings helped firm my resolve. David tried pushing the issue but finally relented and left to walk up around the rock formation to retrieve the gear I had used to build our anchor/belay stance.

"I'll find a couple of sticks for you to use for support," he announced on his return. He quickly found two that would suffice. Then said, "I'll shuttle the packs down the hill."

The sticks helped but what I would have given for the trekking poles down in my car. The process of limping down with my right leg elevated was as expected, a very slow and painful experience. My main enemy was the almost-rotted leaves from the previous fall. They concealed numerous holes and loose rocks in the narrow, deeply eroded climber's path. I slipped and fell twice. Both times I winced and saw white-hot spots beneath my eyelids. While laying on the ground in order to catch my breath I looked up and listened to the rush of the wind coming down off of the top of the bluff through the White Pines like a wave. It helped take my mind off of the pain. Finally I just decided to scoot down the steeper sections. I had to laugh at myself as I began to worry more about ticks than rolling down the slope into a stout tree or large boulder.

At urgent care I learned that an undetected Baker's Cyst had ruptured behind my knee and severely tore my calf muscle. The attending doctor asked me if I wanted a pain prescription and I foolishly refused and said, "I'll just take Advil, it works well enough for me." Well, you know how they always ask you, "What's your level of pain on a scale from one to 10?" Two days later and for a couple more weeks I dealt with excruciating pain that 3200 mg/day of ibuprofen didn't even touch. I now think I know what the pain level of 10 is.

My entire leg eventually turned an ugly blue-black and I had to have a scan to ascertain that a blood clot hadn't developed. I then spent six more weeks living out of my recliner, hobbling around in a steel-braced felt boot on crutches, and going to physical therapy sessions.

THE GOOD: The next year still not convinced that my leg had regained its full strength I needed to know if my calf muscle would last for hours and hours going up and down a real mountain.

That August in South Dakota's Custer State Park after hiking about a mile up the Harney Peak Trail from Sylvan Lake, low clouds began to move in from the west. A little later the ceiling dropped and I found myself moving through an eerie, cool mist with limited visibility. When I arrived at the stone tower – built by the Civilian Conservation Corps in 1934 on Harney's 7,242-foot high summit – it was engulfed in whiteout conditions. I took a picture of the summit plaque and quickly descended back to my car.

The following morning dawned bight and clear. I decided to repeat the hike up Harney. This time from the summit tower I could see parts of three other states (Wyoming, North Dakota, and Nebraska). The only mar on the nearby scenery was the thousands of dead pine trees that had succumbed to a severe infestation of the bark beetle.

That afternoon I drove down to my brother-in-law's in Fort Collins, Colorado. I intended to climb Longs Peak, which at 14,255 feet is the highest peak in Rocky Mountain National Park.

The next morning I reserved a campsite at the Aspenglen Campground, which is located just below the Fall River Entrance to the park. I then drove up Trail Ridge Road to the Alpine Visitor Center to do a yo-yo hike of the four-mile long Ute Trail to further my body's adjustment to the higher altitude. The ancient Indian footpath begins just across the road from the visitor center's parking lot at an elevation of approximately 11,780 feet and eventually drops down to Poudre Lake, which is located at the 10,158-foot high Milner Pass.

I returned three hours later and queried a backcountry ranger for her recommendation for another good acclimatization hike before attempting Longs Peak. "You should hike the three peaks in the Mummy Range," she enthusiastically suggested. She then added, "the views are spectacular and unlike the Keyhole Route on Longs, the hike is relatively deserted on a weekday."

The trailhead for the hike is located at Chapin Creek Pass up on the one-track dirt, Fall River Road. It provides a nice high start for the seven-mile round trip hike that includes the summits of Mt. Chapin (12,454 ft.), Mt. Chiquita (13,069 ft.) and Ypsilon Mountain (13,514 ft.).

The Mummy Range (left to right, Mt. Chapin, Mt. Chiquita and Ypsilon Mountain). (Photo by author)

The next morning I had all three summits to myself – except for a lone cow elk that didn't want to keep me company on top of Mt. Chiquita. And as promised the views were fabulous. From Ypsilon's summit I saw a few other hikers top out on Mt. Chiquita and than turn around. A 50-mph wind out of the northwest likely discouraged them from continuing on to the last and highest peak.

That evening I moved to the Glacier Basin Campground and decided to pass on the hordes that would be attempting Longs Peak. Instead I decided to hike up both Flattop Mountain (12,324 ft.) and Hallett Peak (12,834 ft.) in the morning.

Hallett Peak and Flattop Mountain.
(Photo by author)

The Flattop Mountain Trailhead starts from Bear Lake, and the endless switchbacks to the summit were just as tedious as I remembered from a prior ascent of the mountain with my wife Judy back in 1976.

The worn path leading from Flattop's summit over to Hallett Peak meanders through boulders on the Continental Divide just above Tyndall Glacier. The extremely steep glacier is nestled in its cirque right below the saddle between Hallett and Flattop.

I was quite surprised to find myself alone on top of Hallett Peak. Then, just beyond where I stood on the highest point, my presence was announced by the shrill call of a marmot. I spent the rest of an uninterrupted hour soaking in the sunshine and admiring the magnificent view before returning back to Flattop and slogging down the 4.5-mile descent to Bear Lake and my car.

Author on the Hallett Peak summit.
(Photo by author)

Having soloed seven summits in five days I deemed my leg healed and headed back to my brother-in-law's for a few, good Colorado-craft brews and a delicious, grilled Porkchop dinner.

AND THE ALMOST UGLY: Doug Hempel, whom I first met on the month long Iowa Mountaineer Outing to the European Alps more than 20 years ago invited me to join him on a climb of Longs Peak. Doug's younger than me, extremely fit, and has ascended the coveted 14er 10 times over the past 11 years. Meanwhile, lower back problems kept interrupting my usual routine of hiking, biking and other training needed to prepare myself for the grueling 15-mile round trip endurance hike/climb.

Nevertheless, after another run up Harney Peak and a yo-yo of the Ute Trail, I picked Doug up outside his Estes Park motel at 2:30 a.m., and we began our pre dawn start from the 9,405-foot high Longs Peak Trailhead at about 3:20 a m.

View of Longs Peak and the Diamond (East Face).
(Photo by author)

The well-maintained trail winds up steep switchbacks then proceeds along the top of Mills Moraine to Chasm Junction. From there the trail divides. The standard trail leading to the Keyhole Route heads north (to the right) up to Granite Pass then it continues on up and around the backside of Mount Lady Washington. It ends in the middle of the mile-long Boulder Field, where you then need to cross the boulder-filled terrain to reach the Keyhole. Once you pass through the keyhole the actual climb to the summit begins.

The other trail leaving the junction goes left and gently leads down to where an emergency rock shelter has been constructed below the rocky moraine holding back the pristine waters of Chasm Lake. The lake is located 4.2 miles from the trailhead and sits below in a large cirque at an elevation of 11,758 feet.

Having ascended the standard route to the Keyhole a number of times previously Doug wanted to try a relatively unknown approach to it called the "Camel Couloir." It's an isolated gully located above Chasm Lake that leads up to a pile of rocks on Mount Lady Washington's southwest ridge. The rock pile resembles a kneeling camel. From there it's an easy hike and hop from boulder to boulder down to the Boulder Field and the eventual scramble up to the Keyhole.

Traveling by headlamp above timberline and along the crest of Mills Moraine we saw a portion of the artificially illuminated City of Denver. We reached Chasm Junction about two hours after starting out and took a short break to re-hydrate.

We overtook three other hikers at the rock shelter just below Chasm Lake, and they had thought they were still on the standard trail leading to the Keyhole. I explained to them that they took the wrong turn at the junction. They decided to just follow Doug and me rather than return all the way back to the junction to get back on the normal route.

The five of us scampered up the rocky moraine to the lake and watched the sun began to rise. After taking a couple of pictures of the Alpenglow on the lake and surrounding peaks we quickly made our way along the lake's north shoreline and on up to the base of the remnant, hard-packed snowfield leading down from Mills Glacier.

At that point I began to think we had missed the Camel Couloir in the poor light. But Doug was convinced he remembered reading in a trip report that you need to go all the way to the base of the enormous East Face of Longs Peak to access it.

I was sure that he was misinformed, and we wasted crucial time deciding whether to continue to scramble up towards the sheer 2,000 foot East Face or to descend back towards what looked to be a very steep and loose gully neither of us wanted to tackle.

Doug continuing to ascend towards the Diamond.
(Photo by author)

Finally we continued onward and upward to see if the correct gully was indeed higher up. As we neared the immense East Face, a series of ramps leading up towards the Southwest Slope of Mount Lady Washington looked promising. But I questioned whether the last 100 feet or so required technical gear and a rope to proceed safely. We had neither one with us and Doug had never done any technical climbing.

While Doug and I discussed the possibility of retreating the other three hikers decided to "Give up the Ghost" and turned back.

Right then it got a little brighter out and I noticed a grassy ledge angling up and across the middle of the 1,000-foot wall descending from Mount Lady Washington's southwest ridge. The ledge ended abruptly though adjacent to another couloir that quickly cuts back behind the wall. Having no idea if the gully actually continued to the top or how we were even going to get from the ledge to the start of the gully we decided to give it a go.

Leading the way up I was surprised to find the ledge to be comfortably wide. When I soon spotted three Cairns I yelled down to

191

Doug, "There's three Cairns up here. We're golden now." The Cairns provided a huge lift to us both.

Getting to the gully from the ledge also turned out to be easier than it looked from below. But then we soon ran into some difficult scrambling after the gully cut behind the wall. And, further up the gully narrows significantly and eventually drops over a 15-foot high vertical rock face. Below the top of the obvious dry waterfall I discovered one good handhold, and the only foothold is a small, grass-covered sloping indent tucked well beneath the undercut lip of the rock face.

Hanging by my right hand I placed my left boot toe on the tiny indent and judged the move to get up and over the top of the rock face to be quite difficult. Expecting my hiking boot to skate off of the toehold I pulled up on my right hand and shifted my left palm on a flat, wet area for leverage. Then just as my center of gravity began to drag me back from the wall toward the emptiness beneath me, I was able to launch myself over the top.

Ledge we ascended cuts across the center of the picture and the gully continues up the area in shadow on the right side.
(Photo by Doug Hempel)

Author studying barrier near the top of the gully.
(Photo by Doug Hempel)

I immediately knew I couldn't reverse the move and worried that Doug wouldn't be able to follow me. While he waited below I cautiously continued up the now narrow gully to where it tops out and saw the camel-like formation kneeling about 100 yards farther up the Southwest Slope.

When Doug tried to follow he couldn't bend down enough because of his height to see the small toehold on the undercut rock face. His boots were skating off of the featureless rock below when he yelled, "My arms are beginning to tire!"

I shouted down to him, "Hang on! I'm coming!" I threw off my pack, down-climbed as quickly as I dared and found a small mostly-buried rock to brace my left foot against just above the drop. I then leaned into the rock wall forming the right side of the constricted gully, bent down as far as I dared and was just able to grip his right wrist with my left hand. But it was his best hold and when I grabbed his wrist it threw him off balance.

"Try my left hand," he shouted at me in panic! Two ugly thoughts occurred to me, "What if he begins to pull me off? Will I let go of him? And if he falls what will I tell his wife, Karen?" He would most surely be seriously injured, and should he began to roll it wasn't far to a drop off of several hundred feet.

I calmly grabbed his left wrist and pulled. This time he was able to muscle his way up. "Paul!" he exclaimed in excitement, "Thanks! You just saved my life!"

After slowly ascending the remainder of the gully together we took a well-deserved break before proceeding down to the western end of the Boulder Field. From there we stepped from rock to rock and scrambled up and over the larger boulders up to the Keyhole.

From there the climbing route corkscrews entirely around the upper mountain and is well marked with red and yellow "bull's eyes" painted on the adjacent rocks. Initially they lead you across ledges above the cliffs on the west side of the mountain over and down to the start of about a 500-foot vertical ascent up a broad couloir filled with loose rocks called "The Trough".

Having to dodge rocks kicked down by several inexperienced climbers ascending or descending above you in the big couloir is frightening. I found it ludicrous that Doug and I were the only two climbers that day that had helmets on. Even two backcountry park rangers, who were ascending just ahead of us, only wore NPS ball caps.

It was already getting late and afternoon thunderstorms are a routine threat – especially on Longs. I was relieved when we reached the top of the trough and could finally see the approaching weather coming from the south was still stable.

The next section of the climb called the "The Narrows," is a long traverse above the enormous sheer cliffs on the south side of the mountain. The traverse leads to the bottom of the "The Homestretch," where near vertical polished slabs rise to the summit.

We finally reached the summit at 11:45. We spent 30 minutes there catching our breath before beginning the long descent.

We were halfway across the Boulder Field when it finally started to thunder and rain. The lightening bug fortunately stayed away from us, and we arrived exhausted but safe back at the Trailhead by early evening.

When I described the entire ordeal to my brother-in-law, Dale Crawford, a former native of Portage now living in Fort Collins, he kept asking me, "How old are you?" Apparently, I'm old enough to know better than to ever repeat the experience or am I?

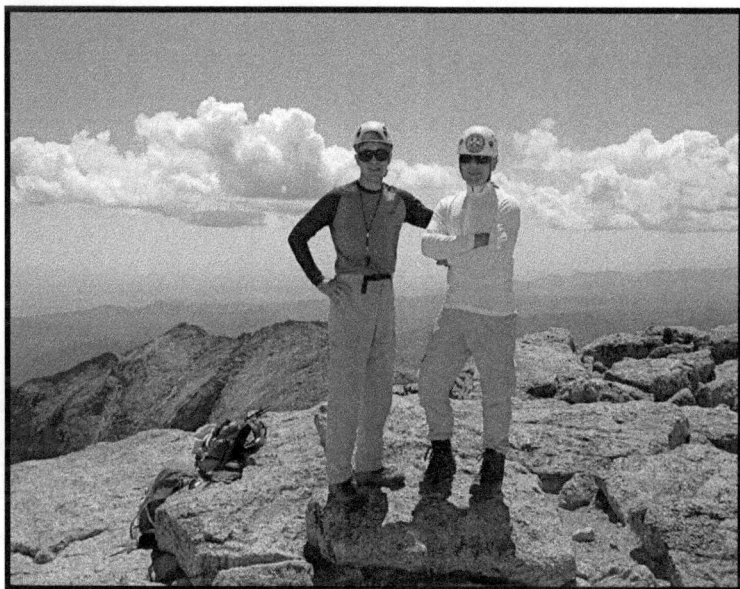

Author and Doug Hempel on Longs Peak summit.
(Photo by unknown Park Ranger).

ONE WRONG TURN,
ONE MISSTEP

Hiking alone in the mountains requires not only lots of mountain sense but spot on judgment. Every single decision you make counts. One wrong turn, one misstep can lead to disastrous consequences.

I had planned to do a Colorado scramble beyond the beaten path up a peak named the Little Matterhorn in Rocky Mountain National Park in 2013.

The unique summit of the Little Matterhorn is the end of the east ridge of Knobtop Mountain and the high point of 11,621 feet is the end of the ridge. The approach leading to near the talus slopes below the ridge is on a good trail. One can either start from the popular Bear Lake parking lot or the Fern Lake Trailhead located at the upper end of Moraine Park. The round-trip distance from either one of the trailheads is about 8.5 miles and generally should take about seven hours.

Unusual, heavy snowfalls in late April and May messed up my plans. I not only didn't bring snowshoes with me but, more importantly, the backcountry park rangers stressed that there was still a fairly high potential for avalanches on the steeper, snow covered slopes above timberline.

Additional risks of hiking in the mountains: a foot or leg injury, lightning, and rock fall. Pine beetles have so decimated the forests out west that the danger of a dead tree falling on you in a high wind has also increased significantly. Encounters with a large predator such as a bear or mountain lion are rare and the likelihood of being attacked by either animal is miniscule, but the possibly does exist—more so when hiking alone. I've seen both of these dangerous predators in the wild. I've also had a rare encounter with a wolverine and several moose have crossed my path in the Teton wilds. I'm not sure the wolverine, which bounded up slope, crossed the Death Canyon trail and continued on up the talus above it was even aware that I was watching it from 50 yards below. A cow moose with a calf can be more dangerous than a bear. The above risks can be pretty much the same whether you're hiking in the mountains alone or in a group. But if something bad happens out there when you're alone, you're on your own and cell reception is usually extremely unreliable.

The weather the first week of June around Estes Park, Colorado was fabulous with clear skies and high temperatures in the 70s.

On June 4, I hiked up the Twin Sisters -- two peaks divided by a narrow saddle. Both peaks are about 11,400 ft. in elevation and I only encountered a few short patches of snow above 10,000 feet. The rocky scramble to the two summits is quite easy and they provide a gorgeous 360-degree view on a clear day. The Twin Sisters Trailhead begins just off of Colorado Highway 7 southeast of Estes Park and the trail gains about 2,400 ft. The entire round trip hike is just 7.8-miles and primarily consists of gentle traverses instead of steep switchbacks. My round-trip time was about four hours.

Two days later I decided to hike to Fern Lake. The round-trip distance is 7.4 miles and I told Judy to expect me back at the Wildwood Inn where we were staying in about four hours.

I left the Fern Lake Trailhead at the end of Moraine Park at 7:30 AM. But when I got up to Fern Lake I decided to follow tracks in the snow up to Odessa Lake, where I knew I could get a good look at the Little Matterhorn. I still planned to climb the peak the next year.

When I reached Odessa Lake I took several pictures and ate my lunch. Then I decided to continue to follow tracks in the snow that pointed out the way up to Lake Helene. From there I knew the same trail eventually descends to Bear Lake, which is located about 3.7 miles from Odessa Lake. I altered my plans because I knew I could catch a hikers shuttle bus back to my car at the Bear Lake parking lot back down to the Fern Lake Trailhead and avoid repeating the 4.4 mile hike back down from Odessa Lake.

The Little Matterhorn above Odessa Lake. (Photo by author)

While traversing some quite steep, snow covered slopes my gut instincts kept telling me to turn around but I ignored the warnings. When I neared Odessa Lake I hiked off trail down to its shoreline to take more pictures. That's when I made another critical error in judgment by forgetting to check behind me for landmarks.

When I tried to relocate the tracks in the snow I had been following earlier I couldn't find them. I did, however, see the basin of Two Rivers Lake through the trees and decided to hike over to it thinking I'd easily pick up the trail near its shoreline.

On my way to Two Rivers Lake the snow no longer supported my weight and I found myself post-holing up to my knees and sometimes all the way up to my waist. When I failed to locate tracks along Two River Lake's shoreline I decided to just follow the out-flowing creek I could hear running beneath the snow. I was sure I would still come across tracks coming up from or descending to Bear Lake.

The timber and brush initially was still sparse just below the lake enabling me to totally avoid walking directly over the snow and ice covered running water. But further below the timberline, interlocking dead branches near the base of adjacent pine trees and thickets of alder along the meandering streambed forced me to occasionally step over or onto it. Three of those times my boots sunk into the snow and punched through the underlying thin ice. And each time the depth of the ice-cold water was just over the tops of my boots. I stopped and emptied the water out of my boots and wrung out my soaked socks.

My feet were quite cold, but with all of the energy I was expending I wasn't worried about freezing my toes as long as I kept moving and had plenty of daylight. I had backup warm layers and the necessary emergency gear in my pack -- including the means to make a warming fire and a thin, foil-coated bivy sack. But in the back of my mind I knew that the mountains could still kill me in a heartbeat.

Lower down I began to run into hidden deadfalls. Vibram boot soles and wet slippery logs are a bad mix. I began slipping and falling over and between logs. Each time I sank in the snow up to my waist or fell over my stamina began to wane. When I got a bad scrape on my right leg and a big bruise on my left knee from breaking through the snow between two dead trees I really began to get concerned that I'd twist an ankle or even break a leg.

I eventually realized I had overshot Bear Lake and just decided to take the Bear Grylls, "Man vs. Wild" advice – "Follow a drainage all the way down to safety." After three hours of hell, which seemed like an eternity, I finally made it to below the snow level, but then I came upon a level flooded meadow that exists on both sides of the stream. It's funny how quickly you abandon your concern and care to keep your boots dry once they're thoroughly wet. I just sloshed right through the soggy ground rather expending the energy to detour around it.

Further down on dry land along the now open creek, just when I began to feel totally safe, I came across a half consumed calf elk carcass propped against a dead pine tree. I was totally spooked and the hair on the back of my neck stood at attention. I found myself looking over my shoulder for a mountain lion or black bear to be stalking me.

A little farther down slope I stumbled upon an old, abandoned trail. For the first time since losing the tracks in snow above Odessa Lake I was smiling. I followed the brushy trail downward to where it eventually intersected with a well-developed trail and I soon met up with a young couple at a footbridge that provides access across the stream I had been following. They informed me that I was at Mill Creek Basin and that I still had about 4.2 miles to go to get to back to my car.

I had cell reception at the log bridge and called Judy to let her know I was safe and would be quite late. The remaining distance to my car didn't concern me as much as I had to climb back up 2.5 miles to where the Mill Creek Trail rises above Cub Lake. Then I had to head down through the area burned by the 2012 Fern Creek fire to where the trail intersects with the Fern Lake Trail at a location called The Pool. From there it's still 1.7 miles to the Fern Creek Trailhead.

I reached my car at 5:30 PM. I arrived back at the resort quite tired, sore, and a little embarrassed. And, of course, I was in a little trouble with my spouse.

Afterwards thinking about my unplanned adventure I realized that I let my guard down, because I've been hiking and climbing in the mountains for the past 40 years. The activities became routine and so familiar that I simply became too over confident.

PAUL HUEBNER

EPILOGUE

C limbing is a very addictive sport. The fitness it demands keeps you feeling young and the outdoor skills you learn provide a boost to your ego. It's actually hard not to begin to feel superior to the average tourists that drive around and stop at view sights to just gawk at wilderness from afar.

But, almost all of my injuries and close calls have occurred while climbing. And I find myself more and more pondering how many times I've "dodged the proverbial bullet." I still shutter when I think about what coulda happened if: that cyst behind my knee woulda ruptured when I was 20 to 30 feet above a bolt, while leading one of the run out climbs in the South Dakota Needles; I failed to wear my helmet or back up my rappel when I had my accident in the North Cascades; or accepted my friend Jerry "Nikko" Cook's offer to join him on his fateful ascent of Mt. Hood.

Then there's all of the short lead falls I've taken over the years, including a 20-footer at Gibraltar Rock in Wisconsin where just a half foot more of rope stretch and I would've probably broken my back on a huge sandstone ledge. I've also had many close calls with a number of the objective hazards in the mountains.

I've asked myself more than once, "What are the odds that I might not be so fortunate in the future?" I even promised myself a long time ago that I'd quit venturing into the mountains when I turned 65. But when I reached that milestone and still had the necessary endurance and strength to repeat a lead of Star Dancer in the Needles behind Mount Rushmore, I told myself, "I should be able to last at least until I'm 80 just like Dave Meyer." But now, right before my 67th birthday and, just as I knew it eventually would, my previous injury to my sacrum has caught up to me. Osteoarthritis has reared its ugly head in the joints between my sacrum and hips.   I always had hoped that hanging up the rope would be more of a voluntary action on my part, instead of due to a past injury. Optimistic I even snapped up a new, dry Mammut 70m rope at the 2013 spring sale at REI.

I now have to face the reality of my age and the consequences of my previous actions. It's depressing! Most of us boomers know "Getting old isn't for sissies."

But life goes on and I'm extremely thankful for all of the companionships and wonderful outdoor experiences I've had the fortune to enjoy. Does anybody need a rope that's never been used? It's still wrapped in its original plastic sheath.

ABOUT THE AUTHOR

Born in 1946, Paul Huebner has lived in Portage, Wisconsin his entire life. After working as a painter with his father, a two-year stint at the local Post Office, and numerous forays in the retail business, he graduated with a B. S. in Natural Resources from the University of Wisconsin—Madison in 1977.

Paul was then a local county's first parks and solid waste manager before accepting a position as a hydrogeologist with the Wisconsin Department of Natural Resources. While working for the Department, he coauthored several technical publications on the site selection, design, construction, operation and monitoring of engineered solid waste landfills and much of the State's current solid waste landfill rules and regulations. He also led the Solid Waste Team for several years and was the Program's liaison with the U. S. Environmental Protection Agency before taking retirement in 2001.

Paul became a recreational rock climber and mountaineer in 1985 at the age of 39. He's ascended peaks in the western United States, Canada, Europe, Mexico, Ecuador and Bolivia to a height of 21,205 feet.

www.ingramcontent.com/pod-product-compliance
Lightning Source LLC
Chambersburg PA
CBHW070350090426
42733CB00009B/1359